Ben Stacy Jerrik (Ed.)

Roe v Minister of Health

Ben Stacy Jerrik (Ed.)

Roe v Minister of Health

Court of Appeal of England and Wales

Part Press

Imprint

Publisher:
Part Press is a trademark of
International Book Market Service Ltd., 17 Rue Meldrum, Beau Bassin, 1713-01 Mauritius
Email: info@bookmarketservice.com
Website: www.bookmarketservice.com

Published in 2011

Printed in: U.S.A., U.K., Germany. This book was not produced in Mauritius.

ISBN: 978-613-7-95498-0

Contents

Articles

References

Roe v Minister of Health

Roe v Minister of Health [1954] 2 All ER 131 is an English tort law decision of the Court of Appeal of England and Wales which has had a significant influence on the common law throughout the common law world.

Facts

Roe and another patient underwent surgery in a hospital managed under the general supervision of the Minister of Health. Before entering the operating theatre, an anaesthetic consisting of Nupercaine was administered by means of a lumbar puncture. At that time, it was common practice to store such anaesthetic in glass ampoules immersed in a phenol solution to reduce the risk of infection. Unknown to the staff, the glass had a number of micro-cracks which were invisible to the eye but which allowed the phenol to penetrate. When used, the phenol-contaminated anaesthetic caused permanent paraplegia.

Judgment

As the law then stood, to find negligence proved, there must be a duty of care, the defendant must have breached that duty, and that breach must have caused the loss or damage sustained by the plaintiff. The standard of care required of defendants was judged by applying an objective test, considering what a "reasonable man" would or would not have done in the same situation. In *Hall v Brooklands Auto Racing Club* (1933) 1 KB 205, it was held that it was the duty of the operators to ensure that the racing track they had designed was as free from danger as reasonable care and skill could make it, but that they were not insurers against accidents which no reasonable diligence could foresee. Similarly, in *Glasgow Corporation v Muir* (1943) 2 AER 44, a defendant was not negligent in allowing a group to enter a tea room to escape bad weather, because the "reasonable man" would not have foreseen that these invitees would injure any of the other customers.

Denning LJ. said, "We must not look at the 1947 incident with 1954 spectacles." It was held that the micro-cracks were not foreseeable given the prevailing scientific knowledge of the time. Thus, since no reasonable anaesthetist would have stored the anaesthetic differently, it was inappropriate to hold the hospital management liable for failing to take precautions. That the profession had changed its practice in the light of experience proved that the profession was responsible in its self-regulation. In 1954, anaesthetists coloured the phenol with a dye. If a vial became contaminated, the dye showed inside the vial. These vials were then discarded. But, given that the hospital was applying the best practice of the time, there was no negligence.

See also

- *Bolam v Friern Hospital Management Committee*
- List of cases involving Lord Denning

Court of Appeal of England and Wales

Court of Appeal	

Royal Courts of Justice, Strand, City of Westminster, London	
Established	1875
Country	England and Wales, UK
Location	Royal Courts of Justice, Strand, City of Westminster, London, UK
Authorized by	HM Government via the Judicature Acts
Decisions are appealed to	Supreme Court of the United Kingdom
Lord Chief Justice of England and Wales	
Currently	Lord Judge
Since	1 October 2008
Jurist term ends	September 2013
Master of the Rolls	
Currently	Lord Dyson
Since	1 October 2012

Her Majesty's Court of Appeal, commonly known as the **Court of Appeal of England and Wales** or, simply, the **Court of Appeal**, is the second most senior court in the English legal system, with only the Supreme Court of the United Kingdom above it. Established in 1875, the Court and its staff of 38 Lord Justices of Appeal hear both criminal appeals in the Criminal Division and civil appeals in the Civil Division, led by the Lord Chief Justice and Master of the Rolls respectively. The Criminal Division hears appeals from the Crown Court, while the Civil Division hears appeals from the County Courts and High Court of Justice. Permission to appeal is required, either from the lower court or the Court of Appeal itself. Decisions may be additionally appealed to the Supreme Court.

History

Formation and early history

The appeal system before 1875 was "chaotic". The superior courts system consisted of 12 different courts, with appeal on common law matters to the Court of Exchequer Chamber, chancery matters to the Court of Appeal in Chancery and other matters to the Privy Council. This was the subject of a review by the Judicature Commission, established in 1867 to consider the creation of a "Supreme Court" (a High Court and Court of Appeal) which was published in 1869. The recommendation was that there should be a common system of appeal from all of the High Court divisions, with a limited set of appeals allowed to the House of Lords.[1] This was instituted by the Judicature Acts, with the Appellate Jurisdiction Act 1876 giving an almost limitless right of appeal to the Lords.[2]

The new legal structure had a single Court of Appeal, split into two divisions, hearing appeals from a unified High Court of Justice made up of the King's Bench, Chancery and Common Pleas Divisions. In its early days, the Court of Appeal divided its sittings between Westminster Hall for appeals from the High Court and Lincoln's Inn for Chancery, Probate, Divorce and Admiralty appeals, with five Lords Justices. After the opening of the Royal Courts of Justice in 1882 they transferred there, where they remain. As well as the Lords Justices, the Lord Chancellor, any previous Lord Chancellors, the Lord Chief Justice, the Lords of Appeal in Ordinary, the Vice-Chancellor of the Chancery Division and the Master of the Rolls could also hear cases, although in practice only the Master of the Rolls did so.[3]

Changes in appellate jurisdiction and procedure

The limitless nature of appeals to the House of Lords was the cause of much concern, involving an additional set of expensive and time-consuming appeals from the Court of Appeal that could not necessarily set decisions down in the knowledge that they were final. The appeals from the County Courts were seen similarly, involving an appeal to the High Court of Justice and the bypassing of the Court of Appeal for a second set of appeals to the Lords. The Administration of Justice (Appeals) Act 1934, a short statute, solved both problems neatly by abolishing the appeal of County decisions to the High Court and instead sending them automatically to the Court of Appeal, and by establishing that appeals to the Lords could only take place with the consent of the Court of Appeal or the Lords themselves.[4]

A second set of changes on appeals took place with the report of the Evershed Committee on High Court Procedure in 1953, which recognised the high cost to the litigants of an additional set of appeals, particularly since the loser in a civil case paid the victor's legal bills. Few changes were made, however, but those enacted included the cessation of the practice that counsel would orally read out the judgment, cross-examinations, documents and evidence given in the lower court, thus cutting time and therefore costs. The process of "leapfrogging" (appealing from the High Court to the House of Lords without needing to go through the Court of Appeal), which they had recommended, was eventually brought into force with the Administration of Justice Act 1969.[5]

In the early 1960s there was an exchange between judges and academics in the United Kingdom and United States comparing the process of appeal used in both nations. Although the British judges found the emphasis on written arguments unattractive, they did like the idea of pre-reading; that the court should read the pleadings of counsel, the case being appealed and the judgment from the lower court before delivering their judgment. After a trial in the Court of Appeal, despite the success of this, the idea was quietly scrapped. The court which Lord Denning presided over from 1962 to 1982 was under no pressure and had no inclination to modernise, with liaisons and management handled by clerks with little knowledge. This changed in 1981 with the appointment of a Registrar, John Adams, an academic and lawyer, who significantly reformed the internal workings of the Court.[6]

The Woolf and Bowman reforms

In July 1996, Lord Woolf published *Access to Justice*, a report on the accessibility of the courts to the public. Woolf identified civil litigation as being categorised by excessive cost, delay and complexity, and managed to replace the diverse rules with a single set of Civil Procedure Rules.[7] Before Woolf had even published his final report, Sir Geoffrey Bowman, a partner at PriceWaterhouseCoopers and former First Parliamentary Counsel, was commissioned to write a report on the Civil Division of the Court of Appeal. Bowman noted a growing workload and delays, with 14 months between setting down and disposing of a case in 70 percent of cases, the rest taking even longer than that – some had taken five years.[8] He recommended extending the requirement to ask leave to appeal to almost all Appeal cases, to allow certain appeals to be heard at a lower level, to focus procedure, impose time limits on oral arguments and move judicial time more towards reading and less towards sitting in court.[9]

Bowman's recommendations were mainly enacted through statutory provisions, such as Part IV of the Access to Justice Act 1999. In *Tanfern Ltd v Cameron-MacDonald* [2000] 1 WLR 1311, Brooke LJ laid down the procedural methods of the Court of Appeal post-Woolf and Bowman. With a few exceptions, such as cases where "the liberty of the subject" is an issue, permission is required to appeal, and may be granted by either the lower court or by the Court of Appeal.[10] As a general rule, appeals are now limited to a review of the decision of the lower court, only allowing a full appeal where there was a serious procedural irregularity or the decision was wrong through "blatant error".[11]

Civil Division

The Civil Division deals with all non-criminal cases, and has been part of the Court since its establishment in 1875. The Civil Division is bound by the Supreme Court of the United Kingdom when making decisions, and is normally bound by its own previous decisions, with four exceptions; where the previous decision was made without the judges knowing of a particular law, where there are two previous conflicting decisions, where there is a later, conflicting Supreme Court or House of Lords decision and where a law was assumed to exist in a previous case but did not. The first three were established by the case of *Young v Bristol Aeroplane Co Ltd* in 1946, the fourth by *R (on the application of Kadhim) v Brent London Borough Housing Benefit Review Board* in 2001.[12] The Civil Division is led by the Master of the Rolls, currently Lord Dyson (who is entitled to the post-nominal MR), assisted by the Vice-President of the Civil Division, Maurice Kay. The division hears cases from the High Court of Justice, County Courts and several tribunals.[13]

Criminal Division

The Criminal Division was established in 1966 with the merger of the Court of Criminal Appeal into the Court of Appeal. It hears all appeals from the Crown Court which are in connection with a trial on indictment (i.e. with a jury) and where the Crown Court has sentenced a defendant committed from the Magistrates' Court. It also exercises the jurisdiction to order the issue of writs of *venire de novo*.[14] The Criminal Division, while bound by the Supreme Court, is more flexible with binding itself, due to the heightened stakes in a case where a possible penalty is a prison sentence.[15] The Division is led by the Lord Chief Justice, currently Lord Judge, assisted by the Vice-President of the Criminal Division, currently Lord Justice Hughes.[16]

Procedure for appeal

Sections 54 to 59 of the Access to Justice Act 1999 and Part 52 of the Civil Procedure Rules 1998 came into force on 2 May 2000, and created one universal appeals system; not all of these are to the Court of Appeal, with the principle used that an appeal should go to the next highest court in the hierarchy.[17] Appeals are allowed if the decision in the court below was incorrect, or suffered from a serious procedural error or irregularity.[18]

Almost all appeals require permission, a major innovation from the previous system, where appeals were, on the request of counsel, almost all automatically put through. The application for permission should be made to the lower court, although this is not mandatory; it may be asked of the appellate court itself. In *Re T (A Child)* [2002] EWCA Civ 1736, the Civil Division strongly advised that counsel apply at the lower courts, since the judge, fully aware of the facts, will take less time to process, there is no harm if the application fails or if it is approved but counsel decides not to proceed with the case and there are no additional costs involved. The only problem here is that judgments may occasionally be reserved, and only given later by post – there may not be an opportunity to ask for permission to appeal at the lower court.[19]

The Court of Appeal, when considering an application for appeal, may decide based on the paper documents or refer the case to an oral hearing, something often done when it is apparent that a refusal of the written case will lead the applicant to send a second, oral application. If a written application is refused, the applicant may ask for an oral hearing to discuss the refusal. Under the Civil Procedure Rules 1998, the appeal must have "a real prospect of success", or there must be "some other compelling reason why the appeal should be heard" for it to be accepted.[20]

Under certain, limited, circumstances, second appeals are allowed. This is when an appeal goes to the High Court or County Court and a party to the case wishes to appeal it further, to the Court of Appeal. Section 55(1) of the Access to Justice Act 1999 says that, when an appeal is made to a County Court or the High Court and that court makes a decision, no further appeal is allowed to the Court of Appeal unless the Court considers that the case raises "an important point of principle or practice" or "there is some other compelling reason for the Court of Appeal to hear it".[21] In *Tanfern Ltd v Cameron-MacDonald* [2000] 1 WLR 1311 the Court commented on this limitation of second appeals, pointing out that the Lords Justices of Appeal were a valuable and scarce resource – it was necessary to impose limitations on appeals to prevent the Court and its judges becoming overburdened.[22]

There are two sorts of hearings that the Court of Appeal can hold; reviews, and full rehearings. Section 52.11(1) of the Civil Procedure Rules 1998 establishes that appeals should always be reviews, unless there are individual circumstances that, "in the interest of justice", make a rehearing necessary.[23] In its case law, the Court has emphasised that it is up to the individual panel of judges to decide whether to hold a review or rehearing, with the circumstances of the case playing a large part.[18] In 2004 the Court heard 1,059 appeals, of which 295 were allowed and 413 directly dismissed.[24]

Judges

The Court of Appeal's main judges are the Lords Justices of Appeal. The Senior Courts Act 1981 provides that the Court of Appeal comprise 38 ordinary sitting Lords Justices and the Lord Chief Justice, Master of the Rolls, President of the Queen's Bench Division, President of the Family Division, and Chancellor of the High Court.[25] Retired Lords Justices sometimes sit in cases, as have retired Law Lords, and High Court judges are allowed to sit on occasion. Lords Justices have, since 1946, been drawn exclusively from the High Court of Justice; prior to this, Lords Justices were (rarely) recruited directly from the Bar.[26] The division of work in the Court of Appeal is demonstrated by the 2005 statistics, in which Lords Justices sat 66% of the time, High Court Judges 26% of the time and Circuit and Deputy High Court Judges 8 per cent of the time.[27] Lord Justices are currently paid £188,900, with the Master of the Rolls paid £205,700 and the Lord Chief Justice £230,400.[28]

The Civil Division is led by the Master of the Rolls, currently Lord Dyson, who uses the postnominal MR; the Chancellor of the High Court and President of the Family Division regularly, for a period of weeks, lead the Civil Division. Several Civil Division Lords Justices are seconded to the Criminal Division, which is currently led by the Lord Chief Justice, Lord Judge.[29]

References

[1] Drewry (2007) p. 31
[2] Drewry (2007) p. 32
[3] Drewry (2007) p. 34
[4] Drewry (2007) p. 35
[5] Drewry (2007) p. 36
[6] Drewry (2007) p. 38
[7] Drewry (2007) p. 46
[8] Drewry (2007) p. 56
[9] Drewry (2007) p. 57
[10] Drewry (2007) p. 58
[11] Drewry (2007) p. 60
[12] Elliott (2008) p. 15
[13] "Going to Court: Court of Appeal" (http://www.judiciary.gov.uk/you-and-the-judiciary/going-to-court/court-of-appeal#headingAnchor2). Judiciary of England and Wales. . Retrieved 28 October 2012.
[14] Senior Courts Act 1981, section 53(2)(d) (http://www.legislation.gov.uk/ukpga/1981/54/section/53-2).
[15] Elliott (2008) p. 16
[16] "Lords Justices of Appeal" (http://www.judiciary.gov.uk/about-the-judiciary/judges-magistrates-and-tribunal-judges/list-of-members-of-the-judiciary/senior-judiciary-list#headingAnchor3). .
[17] Drewry (2007) p. 68

[18] Drewry (2007) p. 81
[19] Drewry (2007) p. 69
[20] Drewry (2007) p. 70
[21] Drewry (2007) p. 71
[22] Drewry (2007) p. 73
[23] Drewry (2007) p. 78
[24] Drewry (2007) p. 84
[25] Senior Courts Act 1981, section 2(1) (http://www.legislation.gov.uk/ukpga/1981/54/section/2).
[26] Drewry (2007) p. 111
[27] Elliott (2008) p. 129
[28] Elliott (2008) p. 139
[29] Drewry (2007) p. 110

Bibliography

- Drewry, Gavin; Louis Bloom-Cooper, Charles Blake (2007). *The Court of Appeal*. Suzanne Fullbrook. Oxford and Portland, Oregon: Hart Publishing. ISBN 1-84113-387-6.
- Elliott, Catherine; Frances Quinn (2008). *English Legal System* (9th ed.). Pearson Longman. ISBN 978-1-4058-5941-7.

External links

- Criminal Division home page (http://www.hmcourts-service.gov.uk/cms/coa_criminal.htm)
- Civil Division home page (http://www.hmcourts-service.gov.uk/cms/civilappeals.htm)

English tort law

English tort law concerns civil wrongs, as distinguished from criminal wrongs, in the law of England and Wales. Some wrongs are the concern of the state, and so the police can enforce the law on the wrongdoers in court – in a criminal case. A tort is not enforced by the police, and it is a civil action taken by one citizen against another, and tried in a court in front of a judge (only rarely, in certain cases of defamation, with a jury). Tort derives from middle English for "injury", from Anglo-French, from Medieval Latin *tortum*, from Latin, neuter of *tortus* "twisted", from past participle of *torquēre*.

History

Following Roman law, the English system has long been based on a closed system of nominate torts, such as trespass, battery and conversion. This is in contrast to the Continental legal systems, which have since adopted more open systems of tortious liability. There are various categories of tort, which lead back to the system of separate causes of action. The tort of negligence is however increasing in importance over other types of tort, providing a wide scope of protection, especially since *Donoghue v Stevenson*. For liability under negligence a duty of care must be established owed to a group of persons of which the victim is one, a nebulous concept into which many other categories are being pulled. But as Lord MacMillan said in the case, "the categories of negligence are never closed".[1]

Negligence

A decomposed snail in Scotland was the humble beginning of the modern law of negligence

Negligence is a tort which targets a breach of duty by one person to another. The famous landmark case of *Donoghue v Stevenson*,[2] in which Mrs Donoghue, the claimant, consumed part of a drink containing a decomposed snail while in a public house in Paisley, Scotland. The snail was not visible, as the bottle of ginger beer in which it was contained was opaque. Neither her friend, who bought it for her, nor the shopkeeper who sold it were aware of its presence. Donoghue sued the manufacturer, Mr Stevenson for her consequent illness, using negligence as, not having purchased the drink herself, the little consumer protection legislation available in 1932 was inapplicable. The members of the House of Lords agreed that Mrs. Donoghue had a valid claim, but disagreed as to why such a claim should exist. Lord MacMillan, as above, thought this should be treated as a new product liability case. Lord Atkin argued that the law should recognise a unifying principle that we owe a duty of reasonable care to our neighbour. He quoted the Bible in support of his argument, specifically the general, biblical principle that "love thy neighbour."

> "The liability for negligence… is no doubt based upon a general public sentiment of moral wrongdoing for which the offender must pay… The rule that you are to love your neighbour becomes in law, you must not injure your neighbour; and the lawyer's question, Who is my neighbour? receives a restricted reply. You must take reasonable care to avoid acts or omissions which you can reasonably foresee would be likely to injure your neighbour."[3]

Thus, in the world of law, he created the doctrine that we should not harm our neighbours. The elements of negligence are:

1. A duty of care (see *Donoghue v Stevenson*)
2. Breach of that duty (see *Nettleship v Weston*)
3. Breach causing harm in fact (see *Smith v Leech Brain & Co.*)
4. The harm must be not too remote a consequence of the breach (see *The Wagon Mound (No. 2)*)

Duty of care

The establishment of a duty of care is, like negligence itself, broken up into further elements, a three step test (or in some cases more). *Donoghue v Stevenson* laid the groundwork for subsequent developments, and from the words of Lord Atkin's speech, he can be seen to refer to firstly, the concept of reasonable foreseeability of harm; secondly, the claimant and the defendant being in a relationship of proximity; and thirdly, and more loosely, it being fair, just and reasonable to impose liability on the defendant for his careless actions. This three step scheme however, did not crystallise until the case of *Caparo Industries Plc v Dickman*.[4] In this somewhat complicated case, a company called Caparo took over another company, by buying up a majority of its shares. It did this because it sneakily obtained word from a company audit that the target was financially sound. The audit was prepared by a group of accountants (Dickman) and was intended for shareholders, not outsiders. Once Caparo owned the company it found that the finances were in fact pretty shoddy, and so it sued the accountants for being negligent in its audit preparation. The House of Lords found against Caparo, and established the current threefold test. Although it was "reasonably foreseeable" that outsiders might learn of the carelessly prepared information, it was not the case that Caparo and Dickman were in a relationship of "proximity". This the court used as a term of art (note, this is different from the American use of the word), to say that it *should* not be the case that absolutely anyone hearing something said that was stupid and acted on it can sue. The court was reacting to its concern that to allow a claim here might open the floodgates of litigation. The third element, whether liability would be "fair, just and reasonable" was an extra hurdle added, as a catch all discretionary measure for the judiciary to block further claims.

Breach of duty

Once a duty of care has been established, it must be shown that a duty has been breached. The question the courts ask is whether the behaviour exhibited by the defendant fell below the threshold of a "reasonable man" (the objective test).[5] In some cases where the defendant was in a special profession, e.g. being a doctor, the court will ask what standard of care a "reasonable doctor" or the like might have done.[6] Allowance is usually made for the defendants age and a lower standard of a "reasonable child of a certain age" is applied to children.[7] On the other hand, no allowance is made for other personal circumstances, such as the fact that the defendant was inexperienced in the task he set out to perform. He is expected to perform this task as a reasonably skilled and competent person.[8]

Causation and remoteness

Causation is complex, and is usually discussed in two parts. Simple causation is a question of whether "but for" the action by the defendant harm would have resulted. There has been some deal of discussion over whether a contributory cause is enough.

- *Barnett v Kensington & Chelsea NHS Trust*
- *McGhee v National Coal Board*
- *Bolitho v City and Hackney Health Authority*
- *Fairchild v Glenhaven Funeral Services Ltd*
- *Gregg v Scott*

After the complexities under the "but for" test have been addressed, the courts may still deny compensation if the harm was a very remote consequence of the initial wrong. So long as a type of damage is foreseeable, however, the manner in which it occurred – however remote – is of no concern to the courts.

- *Scott v Shepherd* (1773) 96 ER 525
- *Re Polemis and Furness, Withy & Co* [1921] 3 KB 560
- *Wagon Mound (No.1)* [1961] AC 388
- *Hughes v Lord Advocate* [1963] AC 837

Defences

Finding a successful defence absolves the defendant from full or partial liability for damages, which makes them valuable commodities in the court. There are three main defences to tortious liability are to argue the claimant voluntarily undertook the risk of his harm, that he contributed to the harm, or that he engaged in illegal activity.

Volenti non fit injuria is Latin for "to the willing, no injury is done". It operates when the claimant either expressly or implicitly consents to the risk of loss or damage. For example, if a regular spectator at an ice hockey match is injured when a player strikes the puck in the ordinary course of play, causing it to fly out of the rink and hit him or her, this is a foreseeable event and regular spectators are assumed to accept that risk of injury when buying a ticket. A slightly more limited defence may arise where the defendant has been given a warning, whether expressly to the plaintiff/claimant or by a public notice, sign or otherwise, that there is a danger of injury. The extent to which defendants can rely on notices to exclude or limit liability varies from country to country. This is an issue of policy as to whether defendants should not only warn of a known danger, but also take active steps to fence the site and take other reasonable precautions to prevent the known danger from befalling those foreseen to be at risk.

Contributory negligence is a mitigatory defence, whereby a claimant's damages are reduced in accordance with the percentage of contribution made by the claimant to the loss or damage suffered. Thus, in evaluating a collision between two vehicles, for example, if the wronged driver were not wearing a seatbelt, he would most likely be contributorily negligent.[9] The court will then quantify the damages for the actual loss or damage sustained, and then reduce the amount paid to the claimant by 20%. Contributory negligence can also function as a full defence, when it is assessed at 100%, as in *Jayes v IMI Kynoch*.[10]

Ex turpi causa non oritur actio is the illegality defence, the Latin for "no right of action arises from a despicable cause". If the claimant is involved in wrongdoing at the time the alleged negligence occurred, this may extinguish or reduce the defendant's liability. Thus, if a burglar is verbally challenged by the property owner and sustains injury when jumping from a second story window to escape apprehension, there is no cause of action against the property owner even though that injury would not have been sustained "but for" the property owner's intervention. However, a trespasser may be able to recover damages due to the unsafe state of the premises (see Occupiers' Liability below).

- *Titchener v British Railways Board*

Psychiatric injury

Historically, English courts have been reluctant to allow claims for nervous shock. Early claims involved ladies who suffered what the courts referred to as a "malady of the mind." It was not expected for men to succumb to such problems.

Today, courts are considerably less cautious but additional hurdles are still imposed upon claimants under certain circumstances. The following criteria must be satisfied:

- The injury must have been an event caused by the defendant – the defendant must have owed a duty of care to the claimant, but not a unilateral duty covering every eventuality, and it must have been precisely identified what duty was owed and whether the harm could have been foreseen.
- The claimant must have been involved in the injury (i.e. proximity must be demonstrated).
- The event must have caused a recognised psychiatric injury (e.g. pathological grief (*Vernon v Bosley* or post-traumatic stress disorder (*Leach v Chief Constable of Gloucestershire*).

The courts had been cautious for a number of reasons, including the fear of floodgates (indeterminate liability), potential for fraud (brought on by people exaggerating their claims), problems of proof and diagnosis (including the costs of expert opinion), psychiatric illness may be considered less serious than physical harm, the claimant is often a secondary victim, and finally, the courts argued that Parliament is better suited to dealing with this area.

But recently, in many cases, it has been recognised that psychiatric injury is more dangerous than physical injury. Claims can arise in a number of circumstances:

Direct Participants

In the case of *Dulieu v White* [1901] 2 KB 669, the claimant, Mrs Dulieu, was working in a public house. While she was serving, the defendant negligently drove his horse-drawn van into the bar. She suffered shock which resulted in a miscarriage, and she sued the defendant. Mr White was held liable for causing nervous shock resulting in miscarriage, as the claimant reasonably believed herself to be in danger.

Similarly, in *Page v Smith* [1995] AC 155, it was held that Mr Smith was liable for causing Mr Page psychiatric injury (chronic fatigue syndrome) after a car crash, because Mr Smith could have reasonably foreseen that Mr Page would suffer physical injury for the crash. So liability for causing psychiatric injury depends on the foreseeability of the physical injury, as long as the psychiatric illness is medically recognised.

In *Young v Charles Church* (Southern LTD)(1997) 39 BMLR 146, the claimant was a "participant" in the event (i.e. a primary victim – Evans & Hitchinson LJJ). He and Mr Cook were raising scaffolding poles in an area that was not secured by the employers; the power lines were not switched off. Mr Cook touched a pole to the electric wiring and suffered a horrific death which caused Mr Young great distress. Even though he never feared for the loss of his own life, the court held that Mr Young was in the area of potential damage, so he was entitled to claim compensation.

Finally, in *McLoughlin v Jones* [2002] QB 1312, there was an allegation that Mr McLoughlin was a bad landlord, threatening and beating up tenants to get their rent from them in cash. He was charged for a criminal offence and sentenced to prison. He claimed that his solicitors (Jones and Others) had acted without the evidence, especially the witness-statement of a person who knew that Mr McLoughlin was not present when the beatings allegedly took place. It soon became apparent that he was actually an upstanding member of society and he suffered psychiatric injury as a result of the imprisonment and loss of reputation. (Note that solicitors have a pre-existing duty of care towards their clients.)

Secondary Victims

The case of *Alcock v Chief Constable of South Yorkshire Police* established a Proximities-Control Device consisting of three stages to establish whether a secondary victim can succeed.

- Foreseeability – there must be a close relationship of love and affection between the secondary victim and the primary victim.
- Proximity – there must be temporal and spatial proximity between the claimant and the accident
- How the accident was caused, or proximity of perception.

Case-law where this test applies includes *McLoughlin v O'Brian* [1983] AC 410, in which the husband and children of the claimant were involved in a car accident that was caused by the negligence of the defendant. The claimant found out about the accident an hour later and, when she got to the hospital two hours later, one child had already died. She saw her husband and children suffering and suffered shock, depression and a change of personality. The court established a spectrum of proximity; a pedestrian should be able to withstand seeing the accidents that occur in everyday life, but a family member of the victims will inevitably suffer greater emotional harm. Nonetheless, simply seeing the aftermath of the accident and not witnessing it is insufficient proximity. Similarly, seeing a video of the accident is insufficient.

Alcock v Chief Constable of South Yorkshire Police (1992) HL was a 'test' case in the aftermath of the Hillsborough disaster, where 95 spectators were crushed to death and 400 injured in a stadium. The event was televised and broadcast on radio. In Alcock, claims for damages for psychiatric illness were brought by fifteen relatives of the victims of the tragedy; some of them had been present at the match - but not in the area where the disaster occurred - and others had seen it on television or heard it on the radio. The Chief Constable of South Yorkshire Police denied that he owed the claimants a duty of care. On the basis of the three principles mentioned above, all claims were ruled out.

Pure economic loss

- *Spartan Steel & Alloys Ltd v Martin & Co (Contractors) Ltd* [1973] QB 27
- *Murphy v Brentwood District Council* [1991] 1 AC 398
- *Aswan Engineering Establishment Co v Lupdine Ltd* [1987] 1 WLR 1
- *Smith v Eric S Bush* [1990] 1 AC 831

Public bodies

- *Anns v Merton London Borough Council*
- *Home Office v Dorset Yacht*

Omissions and third parties

- *Smith v Littlewoods Organisation Ltd*

Specific torts

Product liability

In consumer protection, with the *Product Liability Directive* in the European Union, where businesses making defective products that harm people must pay for any damage resulting. Liability for defective products is strict (see strict liability) in most jurisdictions. The theory of risk spreading provides support for this approach. Since manufacturers are the 'cheapest cost avoiders', because they have a greater chance to seek out problems, it makes sense to give them the incentive to guard against product defects.

Occupiers' Liability

Occupiers' Liability is another example. Governed by the Occupier's Liability Acts, 1956 and 1984 whereby an occupier, such as a shop owner, who invites others onto land, or has trespassers, owes a minimum duty of care for people's safety. One early case was *Cooke v Midland Great Western Railway of Ireland* [1909] AC 229, in which Lord Macnaughton felt that children who were hurt whilst looking for berries on a building site, should have some compensation for their unfortunate curiosity.

- *Roles v Nathan*
- *Tomlinson v Congleton Borough Council*

Other statutory torts

Other statutory torts can be found in regulation concerning food safety, health and safety and environmental law. For example, liability under the Nuclear Installations Act 1965, the Merchant Shipping Act 1995, or liability imposed on utility (gas and electricity) companies to ensure the safety of their products, all of which are strict liability.[11] While a statute has said nothing specific, a tortious duty may have arisen. This will be a question of statutory interpretation (e.g. *Stovin v Wise* [1996] AC 923).

Nuisance

The tort of nuisance allows a claimant (formerly plaintiff) to sue for most acts that interfere with their use and enjoyment of their land. A good example of this is in the case of *Jones v Powell* (1629).[12] A brewery made stinking vapors waft to neighbors' property, damaging his papers. Because he was a landowner, the neighbor sued in nuisance for this damage. But Whitelocke J, speaking for the Court of the King's Bench, said that because the water supply was contaminated, it was better that the neighbor's documents were risked. He said "it is better that they should be spoiled than that the common wealth stand in need of good liquor." Nowadays, interfering with neighbors' property is not looked upon so kindly. Nuisance deals with all kinds of things that spoil a landowner's enjoyment of his property.

- *Sturges v Bridgman*
- *Miller v Jackson*

Rylands v Fletcher

A subset of nuisance is known as the rule in *Rylands v Fletcher*[13] where a dam burst into a coal mine shaft. So a dangerous escape of some hazard, including water, fire, or animals means strict liability in nuisance. This is subject only to a remoteness cap, familiar from negligence when the event is unusual and unpredictable. This was the case where chemicals from a factory seeped through a floor into the water table, contaminating East Anglia's reservoirs.[14]

Trespass

A trespass is a direct injury to a person, his property or land, committed directly and intentionally by the defendant, for example, walking on someone's land or cutting a gate into pieces with a saw. However, this rule did not cater for anything injured indirectly by a person, for example if a farmer sets fire to a field, and someone's home is subsequently damaged. Trespass by the case did, however, provide a legal writ for injury caused indirectly by an action.

Defamation

Defamation means tarnishing the reputation of someone. It is divided into two parts, slander and libel. Slander is spoken defamation and libel is defaming somebody through print (or broadcasting). Both share the same features. To defame someone, you must (a) make a factual assertion (b) for which you cannot provide evidence of its truth. Defamation does not affect the voicing of opinions, but comes into the same fields as rights to free speech in the European Convention's Article 10.

Intentional torts

Intentional torts are any intentional acts that are reasonably foreseeable to cause harm to an individual, and that do so. Intentional torts have several subcategories, including tort(s) against the person, including assault, battery, false imprisonment, intentional infliction of emotional distress, and fraud. Property torts involve any intentional interference with the property rights of the claimant. Those commonly recognised include trespass to land, trespass to chattels, and conversion.

- *Derry v Peek*

Economic torts and competition

Strikers gathering in Tyldesley in the 1926 General Strike in the U.K.

Economic torts protect people from interference with their trade or business. The area includes the doctrine of restraint of trade and has largely been submerged in the twentieth century by statutory interventions on collective labour law and modern antitrust or competition law. The "absence of any unifying principle drawing together the different heads of economic tort liability has often been remarked upon."[15]

Two cases demonstrated economic tort's affinity to competition and labour law. In *Mogul Steamship Co. Ltd.*[16] the plaintiff argued he had been driven from the Chinese tea market by competitors at a 'shipping conference' that had acted together to underprice his company. But this cartel was ruled lawful and "nothing more [than] a war of competition waged in the interest of their own trade."[17] Nowadays, this would be considered a criminal cartel. In labour law the most notable case is *Taff Vale Railway Co v Amalgamated Society of Railway Servants*.[18] The House of Lords thought that unions should be liable in tort for helping workers to go on strike for better pay and conditions, but it riled workers so much that it led to the creation of the British Labour Party and the Trade Disputes Act 1906. Further torts used against unions include conspiracy,[19] interference with a commercial contract[20] or intimidation.[21]

Through a recent development in common law, beginning with *Hedley Byrne v Heller*[22] in 1964, and further through the Misrepresentations Act 1967, a victim of the tort[23] of misrepresentation will be compensated for purely economic loss due to the misconception of the terms of the contract.

The English doctrine of restraint of trade was the catalyst for much of what is now called "competition laws" (or sometimes "antitrust"). These laws are a way of restraining those who would restrain "free competition" in the market economy, through monopolising production, setting up cartels, imposing unfair trading conditions, prices and so on. The English approach has traditionally been very flexible and liberal in its scope, but draconian when it did deem certain behaviour to be in restraint of trade. Many of these laws around the end of the nineteenth century were focused on the emasculation of trade unionism, until the reforming government of 1906 and the Trade Disputes Act 1906. Aside from the common law, legislation was introduced shortly after the second world war to foot policy on a statutory basis, the Monopolies and Restrictive Practices Act 1948, followed later by the Restrictive Trade Practices Act 1956 and the Monopolies and Mergers Act 1965.

Since 1972 however, the U.K. fell under the cross-border competition law regime of the European Community, which is found primarily in Articles 81 and 82 of the Treaty of the European Community. Companies who form a cartel or collude to disrupt competition (Article 81) or abuse a dominant position on the market, for instance through a monopoly (Article 82) face fines from the public enforcement authorities, and in some cases a cause of action in tort, for the purposes of private enforcement may arise. A huge issue in the E.U. is whether to follow the U.S. approach of private damages actions to prevent anti-competitive conduct.[24] In other words, the question is what should be seen as a private wrong (as was held in the vertical restraints case of *Courage Ltd v Crehan*[25]) and what should be seen as a public wrong where only public enforcers are competent to impose penalties. In 1998 the United Kingdom brought its legislation up to date, with the Competition Act 1998, followed by the Enterprise Act 2002, a regime mirroring that of the European Union. The domestic enforcers are the Office of Fair Trading and the Competition Commission.

Vicarious liability

"If a slave man or woman damages any piece of someone else's property, then provided the person who suffers the loss was not himself partly to blame because of inexperience or careless conduct, the slave's owner must either make good the damage in full, or hand over the actual offender."
Plato, *The Laws*, Book 11, §25, Damage by slaves.

Vicarious liability refers to the idea of an employer being liable for torts committed by their employees, generally for policy reasons, and to ensure that victims have a means of recovery.[26] The word "vicarious" derives from the Latin for 'change' or 'alternation'[27] and the old Latin for the doctrine is *respondeat superior*. To establish vicarious liability, the courts must find first that there exists a relationship of employee and employer. The torts of independent contractors generally do not impose vicarious liability on employers; however, *Honeywill and Stein Ltd v Larkin Brothers Ltd* demonstrates this principle does not apply where particularly hazardous activities are contracted for, or a non-delegable duty is owed. Secondly, the tort must have been committed 'in the course of employment'; or while an employee is going about the business of their employer. A preferred test of the courts for connecting torts to the course of employment was formulated by John William Salmond, which states that an employer will be held liable for either a wrongful act they have authorised, or a wrongful and unauthorised mode of an act that was authorised.[28] Where in *Limpus v London General Omnibus Company* an omnibus driver chose to disobey strict instructions from his employer, to obstruct a rival company, they were still liable, as he was merely engaging in his duties in an unauthorised way. However, in the contrasting case of *Beard v London General Omnibus Company*, there was no liability where a conductor drove an omnibus negligently, as it was no part of his duties. Under the test, employers were generally not held liable for intentional torts of their employees. *Lister v Hesley Hall Ltd* established a newer test, stating that employers would be liable for torts which were *closely connected* to the duties of an employee.

Remedies

Damages

The main remedy against tortious loss is compensation in 'damages' or money. In a limited range of cases, tort law will tolerate self-help, such as reasonable force to expel a trespasser. This is a defence against the tort of battery. Further, in the case of a continuing tort, or even where harm is merely threatened, the courts will sometimes grant an injunction. This means a command, for something other than money by the court, such as restraining the continuance or threat of harm.[29]

For people who have died as a result of another person's tort, the damages that their estate or their families may gain is governed by the Fatal Accidents Act 1976 (replacing the Fatal Accidents Act 1846). Under s.1A the spouse or dependent of a victim may receive £11,800[30] in bereavement damages.

Injunctions

As a remedy to tort, injunctions are most commonly used in cases of Nuisance. The court may impose an injunction on a tortfeasor, such as in Sturges v Bridgman. This legally obliges the tortfeasor to stop or reduce the activity causing the nuisance and its breach could, potentially, be a criminal offence. Injunctions may be used instead of or as well as the awarding of damages (above).

Theory and reform

Scholars and lawyers have identified conflicting aims for the law of tort, to some extent reflected in the different types of damages awarded by the courts: compensatory, aggravated and punitive or exemplary. In *The Aims of the Law of Tort* (1951),[31] Glanville Williams saw four possible bases on which different torts rested: appeasement, justice, deterrence and compensation.

From the late 1950s a group of legally oriented economists and economically oriented lawyers emphasised incentives and deterrence, and identified the aim of tort as being the efficient distribution of risk. They are often described as the *law and economics movement*. Ronald Coase, one of the movement's principal proponents, submitted, in his article *The Problem of Social Cost* (1960),[32] that the aim of tort should be to reflect as closely as possible liability where transaction costs should be minimised.

Calls for reform of tort law come from diverse standpoints reflecting diverse theories of the objectives of the law. Some calls for reform stress the difficulties encountered by potential claimants. Because of all people who have accidents, only some can find solvent defendants from which to recover damages in the courts, P. S. Atiyah has called the situation a "damages lottery".[33] Consequently, in New Zealand, the government in the 1960s established a "no-fault" system of state compensation for accidents. Similar proposals have been the subject of Command Papers in the UK and much academic debate.

There is some overlap between crime and tort, since tort, a private action, used to be used more than criminal laws in centuries gone. For example, an assault is both a crime and a tort (a form of trespass to the person). A tort allows a person, usually the victim, to obtain a remedy that serves their own purposes (for example by the payment of damages to a person injured in a car accident, or the obtaining of injunctive relief to stop a person interfering with their business). Criminal actions on the other hand are pursued not to obtain remedies to assist a person — although often criminal courts do have power to grant such remedies — but to remove their liberty on the state's behalf. That explains why incarceration is usually available as a penalty for serious crimes, but not usually for torts.

See also

- English contract law
- Insurance law
- Law
- Jurisprudence

Notes

[1] [1932] AC 563, 561
[2] [1932] AC 562
[3] *Donoghue v Stevenson* [1932] A.C. 532, 580
[4] *Caparo Industries plc v Dickman* [1990] Full text from BaiLII.org UKHL 2 (http://www.bailii.org/uk/cases/UKHL/1990/2.html)
[5] *Blyth v Company Proprietors of the Birmingham Water Works* (1856) 11 Ex Ch 781
[6] *Bolam v Friern Hospital Management Committee[1957] 2 All ER 118*
[7] *Mullin v Richards* [1998] 1 All ER 920
[8] *Nettleship v Weston* [1971] 3 All ER 581, *Wells v Cooper* (1958) 2 All ER 527
[9] http://www.compactlaw.co.uk/legal_glossary/c/contributory_negligence.html
[10] [1985] ICR 155

[11] http://www.legal500.com/books/l500/developments/144
[12] *Jones v Powell* (1629) 123 Eng. Rep. 1155
[13] *Rylands v Fletcher* (1866) LR 1 Exch 265
[14] Cambridge Water Co Ltd v Eastern Counties Leather plc [1994] 2 AC 264
[15] p.509 *Markesinis and Deakin's Tort Law* (2003 5th Ed.) OUP)
[16] *Mogul Steamship Co Ltd v McGregor, Gow & Co* (1889) LR 23 QBD 598
[17] per Bowen LJ, (1889) LR 23 QBD 598, 614
[18] *Taff Vale Railway Co v Amalgamated Society of Railway Servants* [1901] AC 426
[19] *Quinn v Leatham* [1901] AC 495
[20] *Torquay Hotels Ltd v Cousins* [1968]
[21] *Rookes v Barnard* [1964] AC 1129
[22] [1964] AC 465
[23] Although this area of law clearly overlaps with contract, misrepresentation is a tort as confirmed by Bridge LJ in *Howard Marine and Dredging Co. Ltd. v A Ogden & Sons* [1978] QB 574
[24] Richard Whish, Competition Law (2003) 5th Ed., Lexis Nexis, Ch. 10
[25] C-453/99 *Courage Ltd v Crehan* [2002] ICR 457
[26] Steele, Jenny (2007). *Tort Law: Text, Cases, & Materials*. Oxford University Press. ISBN 0-19-924885-0., p. 567
[27] vicarious – Definition from the Merriam–Webster Online Dictionary (http://www.m-w.com/dictionary/vicarious)
[28] Heuston, R.E.V.; Buckley, R.A. (1996). *Salmond and Heuston on the Law of Torts*. Sweet & Maxwell. ISBN 0-421-53350-1., p. 443
[29] Miller v Jackson [1975]
[30] see, SI 2007/3489 Damages for Bereavement (Variation of Sums) (England and Wales) Order) Art.2
[31] Williams, G. [1951] "The Aims of the Law of Tort", *Current Legal Problems* 137
[32] Coase, R. H. (1960). "The Problem of Social Cost". *The Journal of Law and Economics* **3** (1): 1–44. doi:10.1086/466560., repreinted in Coase, R. H. (1990). *The Firm, the Market and the Law*. Chicago: Chicago University Press. pp. *pp*95–156. ISBN 0-226-11101-6., online version (http://www.sfu.ca/~allen/CoaseJLE1960.pdf)
[33] Atiyah, P. S. (1997) *The Damages Lottery*

References

- S Deakin, A Johnston and B Markesinis, *Tort Law* (2003) 5th Ed. Oxford University Press, ISBN 0-19-925711-6
- M Lunney, K Oliphant, *Tort Law – Texts, Cases* (2003) 2nd Ed. Oxford University Press, ISBN 0-19-926055-9
- *Cases, Materials and Text on National, Supranational and International Tort Law* ISBN 1-84113-139-3

Common law

Common law, also known as **case law** or **precedent**, is law developed by judges through decisions of courts and similar tribunals, as opposed to statutes adopted through the legislative process or regulations issued by the executive branch.[1]

A "common law system" is a legal system that gives great precedential weight to common law,[2] on the principle that it is unfair to treat similar facts differently on different occasions.[3] The body of precedent is called "common law" and it binds future decisions. In cases where the parties disagree on what the law is, a common law court looks to past precedential decisions of relevant courts. If a similar dispute has been resolved in the past, the court is bound to follow the reasoning used in the prior decision (this principle is known as *stare decisis*). If, however, the court finds that the current dispute is fundamentally distinct from all previous cases (called a "matter of first impression"), judges have the authority and duty to make law by creating precedent.[4] Thereafter, the new decision becomes precedent, and will bind future courts.

In practice, common law systems are considerably more complicated than the simplified system described above. The decisions of a court are binding only in a particular jurisdiction, and even within a given jurisdiction, some courts have more power than others. For example, in most jurisdictions, decisions by appellate courts are binding on lower courts in the same jurisdiction and on future decisions of the same appellate court, but decisions of lower courts are only non-binding persuasive authority. Interactions between common law, constitutional law, statutory law and regulatory law also give rise to considerable complexity. However, *stare decisis*, the principle that similar cases should be decided according to consistent principled rules so that they will reach similar results, lies at the heart of all common law systems.

One third of the world's population (approximately 2.3 billion people) live in common law jurisdictions or in systems mixed with civil law. Particularly common law is in England where it originated in the Middle Ages,[5] and in countries that trace their legal heritage to England as former colonies of the British Empire, including India,[6] the United States, Pakistan,[7] Nigeria, Bangladesh, Canada, with the exception of Québec where a mix of civil law (on the provincial level) and common law (mostly on the federal level) is used, Malaysia, Ghana, Australia,[8] Sri Lanka, Hong Kong, Singapore,[9] Myanmar, Ireland, New Zealand, Jamaica, Trinidad and Tobago, Cyprus, Barbados,[10] South Africa, Zimbabwe, Cameroon, Namibia, Botswana, Guyana and Israel.

Primary connotations

The term *common law* has three main connotations and several historical meanings worth mentioning:

Common law as opposed to statutory law and administrative/regulatory law

Connotation 1 distinguishes the authority that promulgated a law. For example, most areas of law in most Anglo-American jurisdictions include "statutory law" enacted by a legislature, "regulatory law" promulgated by executive branch agencies pursuant to delegation of rule-making authority from the legislature, and common law or "case law", *i.e.*, decisions issued by courts (or quasi-judicial tribunals within agencies).[11] [12] This first connotation can be further differentiated into (a) pure common law arising from the traditional and inherent authority of courts to define what the law is, even in absence of an underlying statute, *e.g.*, most criminal law and procedural law before the 20th century, and even today, most of contract law and the law of torts, and (b) court decisions that interpret and decide the fine boundaries and distinctions in law promulgated by other bodies. This body of common law, sometimes called "interstitial common law," includes judicial interpretations of the Constitution, of statutes, and of regulations, and examples of application of law to facts.[13]

Common law legal systems as opposed to civil law legal systems

Connotation 2 differentiates "common law" jurisdictions and legal systems from "civil law" or "code" jurisdictions.[13] Common law systems place great weight on court decisions, which are considered "law" with the same force of law as statutes—for nearly a millennium, common law courts have had the authority to make law where no legislative statute exists, and statutes mean what courts interpret them to mean. By contrast, in civil law jurisdictions (the legal tradition that prevails, or is combined with common law, in Europe and most non-Islamic, non-common law countries), courts lack authority to act where there is no statute, and judicial precedent is given less interpretive weight (which means that a judge deciding a given case has more freedom to interpret the text of a statute independently, and less predictably), and scholarly literature is given more. For example, the Napoleonic code expressly forbade French judges to pronounce general principles of law.[14]

As a rule of thumb, common law systems trace their history to England, while civil law systems trace their history to Roman law and the Napoleonic Code.

The contrast between common law and civil law systems is elaborated in "Contrasts between common law and civil law systems" and "Alternatives to common law systems", below.

Law as opposed to equity

Connotation 3 differentiates "common law" (or just "law") from "equity".[11] [12] Before 1873, England had two parallel court systems: courts of "law" that could only award money damages and recognized only the legal owner of property, and courts of "equity" (courts of chancery) that could issue injunctive relief (that is, a court order to a party to do something, give something to someone, or stop doing something) and recognized trusts of property. This split propagated to many of the colonies, including the United States (see "Reception Statutes", below). For most purposes, most jurisdictions, including the U.S. federal system and most states, have merged the two courts.[15] [16] Additionally, even before the separate courts were merged, most courts were permitted to apply both law and equity, though under potentially different procedural law. Nonetheless, the historical distinction between "law" and "equity" remains important today when the case involves issues such as the following:

- categorizing and prioritizing rights to property—for example, the same article of property often has a "legal title" and an "equitable title," and these two groups of ownership rights may be held by different people.
- in the United States, determining whether the Seventh Amendment's right to a jury trial applies (a determination of a fact necessary to resolution of a "common law" claim)[17] or whether the issue will be decided by a judge (issues of what the law is, and all issues relating to equity).
- the standard of review and degree of deference given by an appellate tribunal to the decision of the lower tribunal under review (issues of law are reviewed *de novo*, that is, "as if new" from scratch by the appellate tribunal, while most issues of equity are reviewed for "abuse of discretion," that is, with great deference to the tribunal below).
- the remedies available and rules of procedure to be applied.

Historical uses

In addition, there are several historical uses of the term that provide some background as to its meaning.

In one archaic usage, "common law" is used to refer to certain customs in England dating to before the Norman conquest and before there was any consistent law to be applied.[18] [19] This definition is found or alluded to in some internet dictionaries,[20] but this definition is unhelpful, because it is both underinclusive and overinclusive.[21]

The English Court of Common Pleas dealt with lawsuits in which the Monarch had no interest, i.e., between commoners.

Additionally, from at least the 11th century and continuing for several centuries after that, there were several different circuits in the royal court system, served by itinerant judges who would travel from town to town dispensing the King's justice. The term "common law" was used to describe the law held in common between the circuits and the different stops in each circuit. The more widely a particular law was recognized, the more weight it held, whereas purely local customs were generally subordinate to law recognized in a plurality of jurisdictions.

These definitions are archaic, their relevance having dissipated with the development of the English legal system over the centuries, but they do explain the origin of the term as used today.

Basic principles of common law

Common law adjudication

In a common law jurisdiction several stages of research and analysis are required to determine "what the law is" in a given situation. First, one must ascertain the facts. Then, one must locate any relevant statutes and cases. Then one must extract the principles, analogies and statements by various courts of what they consider important to determine how the next court is likely to rule on the facts of the present case. Later decisions, and decisions of higher courts or legislatures carry more weight than earlier cases and those of lower courts.[22] Finally, one integrates all the lines drawn and reasons given, and determines "what the law is". Then, one applies that law to the facts.

The common law evolves to meet changing social needs and improved understanding

Justice Holmes cautioned that "the proper derivation of general principals in both common and constitutional law ... arise gradually, in the emergence of a consensus from a multitude of particularized prior decisions."[23] Justice Cardozo noted the "common law does not work from pre-established truths of universal and inflexible validity to conclusions derived from them deductively," but "[i]ts method is inductive, and it draws its generalizations from particulars."[24]

The common law is more malleable than statutory law. First, common law courts are not absolutely bound by precedent, but can (when extraordinarily good reason is shown) reinterpret and revise the law, without legislative intervention, to adapt to new trends in political, legal and social philosophy. Second, the common law evolves through a series of gradual steps, that gradually works out all the details, so that over a decade or more, the law can change substantially but without a sharp break, thereby reducing disruptive effects.[25] In contrast to common law incrementalism, the legislative process is very difficult to get started, as legislatures tend to delay action until a situation is totally intolerable. For these reasons, legislative changes tend to be large, jarring and disruptive (sometimes positively, sometimes negatively, and sometimes with unintended consequences).

One example of the gradual change that typifies the common law is the gradual change in liability for negligence. For example, the traditional common law rule through most of the 19th century was that a plaintiff could not recover for a defendant's negligent production or distribution of a harmful instrumentality unless the two were in privity of contract. Thus, only the immediate purchaser could recover for a product defect, and if a part was built up out of parts from parts manufacturers, the ultimate buyer could not recover for injury caused by a defect in the part. In an 1842 English case, *Winterbottom v. Wright*,[26] the postal service had contracted with Wright to maintain its coaches. Winterbottom was a driver for the post. When the coach failed and injured Winterbottom, he sued Wright. The *Winterbottom* court recognized that there would be "absurd and outrageous consequences" if an injured person could sue any person peripherally involved, and knew it had to draw a line somewhere, a limit on the causal connection between the negligent conduct and the injury. The court looked to the contractual relationships, and held that liability would only flow as far as the person in immediate contract ("privity") with the negligent party.

A first exception to this rule arose in an 1852 case by New York's highest court, *Thomas v. Winchester*,[27] which held that mislabeling a poison as an innocuous herb, and then selling the mislabeled poison through a dealer who would be expected to resell it, put "human life in imminent danger." *Thomas* used this as a reason to create an exception to the "privity" rule. In, 1909, New York held in *Statler v. Ray Mfg. Co.*[28] that a coffee urn manufacturer was liable to a person injured when the urn exploded, because the urn "was of such a character inherently that, when applied to the purposes for which it was designed, it was liable to become a source of great danger to many people if not carefully and properly constructed."

Yet the privity rule survived. In *Cadillac Motor Car Co. v. Johnson*,[29] (decided in 1915 by the federal appeals court for New York and several neighboring states), the court held that a car owner could not recover for injuries from a defective wheel, when the automobile owner had a contract only with the automobile dealer and not with the manufacturer, even though there was "no question that the wheel was made of dead and 'dozy' wood, quite insufficient for its purposes." The *Cadillac* court was willing to acknowledge that the case law supported exceptions for "an article dangerous in its nature or likely to become so in the course of the ordinary usage to be contemplated by the vendor." However, held the *Cadillac* court, "one who manufactures articles dangerous only if defectively made, or installed, e.g., tables, chairs, pictures or mirrors hung on the walls, carriages, automobiles, and so on, is not liable to third parties for injuries caused by them, except in case of willful injury or fraud,"

Finally, in the famous case of *MacPherson v. Buick Motor Co.*,[30] in 1916, Judge Benjamin Cardozo for New York's highest court pulled a broader principle out of these predecessor cases. The facts were almost identical to *Cadillac* a year earlier: a wheel from a wheel manufacturer was sold to Buick, to a dealer, to MacPherson, and the wheel failed, injuring MacPherson. Judge Cardozo held:

> It may be that Statler v. Ray Mfg. Co. have extended the rule of Thomas v. Winchester. If so, this court is committed to the extension. The defendant argues that things imminently dangerous to life are poisons, explosives, deadly weapons—things whose normal function it is to injure or destroy. But whatever the rule in Thomas v. Winchester may once have been, it has no longer that restricted meaning. A scaffold (Devlin v. Smith, supra) is not inherently a destructive instrument. It becomes destructive only if imperfectly constructed. A large coffee urn (Statler v. Ray Mfg. Co., supra) may have within itself, if negligently made, the potency of danger, yet no one thinks of it as an implement whose normal function is destruction. What is true of the coffee urn is equally true of bottles of aerated water (Torgeson v. Schultz, 192 N. Y. 156). We have mentioned only cases in this court. But the rule has received a like extension in our courts of intermediate appeal. In Burke v. Ireland (26 App. Div. 487), in an opinion by CULLEN, J., it was applied to a builder who constructed a defective building; in Kahner v. Otis Elevator Co. (96 App. Div. 169) to the manufacturer of an elevator; in Davies v. Pelham Hod Elevating Co. (65 Hun, 573; affirmed in this court without opinion, 146 N. Y. 363) to a contractor who furnished a defective rope with knowledge of the purpose for which the rope was to be used. We are not required at this time either to approve or to disapprove the application of the rule that was made in these cases. It is enough that they help to characterize the trend of judicial thought.
>
> We hold, then, that the principle of *Thomas v. Winchester* is not limited to poisons, explosives, and things of like nature, to things which in their normal operation are implements of destruction. If the nature of a thing is such that it is reasonably certain to place life and limb in peril when negligently made, it is then a thing of danger. Its nature gives warning of the consequences to be expected. If to the element of danger there is added knowledge that the thing will be used by persons other than the purchaser, and used without new tests then, irrespective of contract, the manufacturer of this thing of danger is under a duty to make it carefully. ... There must be knowledge of a danger, not merely possible, but probable.

Cardozo's new "rule" exists in no prior case, but is inferrable as a synthesis of the "thing of danger" principle stated in them, merely extending it to "foreseeable danger" even if "the purposes for which it was designed" were not themselves "a source of great danger." *MacPherson* takes some care to present itself as foreseeable progression, not a wild departure. Cardozo continues to adhere to the original principle of *Winterbottom*, that "absurd and outrageous consequences" must be avoided, and he does so by drawing a new line in the last sentence quoted above: "There must be knowledge of a danger, not merely possible, but probable." But while adhering to the underlying principle that *some* boundary is necessary, *MacPherson* overruled the prior common law by rendering the formerly dominant factor in the boundary, that is, the privity formality arising out of a contractual relationship between persons, totally irrelevant. Rather, the most important factor in the boundary would be the nature of the thing sold and the foreseeable uses that downstream purchasers would make of the thing.

This illustrates two crucial principles that are often not well understood by non-lawyers. (a) The law evolves, this evolution is in the hands of judges, and judges have "made law" for hundreds of years. (b) The reasons given for a decision are often more important in the long run than the outcome in a particular case. This is the reason that judicial opinions are usually quite long, and give rationales and policies that can be balanced with judgment in future cases, rather than the bright-line rules usually embodied in statutes.

Interaction of constitutional, statutory and common law

In common law legal systems (connotation 2), the common law (connotation 1) is crucial to understanding almost all important areas of law. For example, in England and Wales and in most states of the United States, the basic law of contracts, torts and property do not exist in statute, but only in common law (though there may be isolated modifications enacted by statute). As another example, the Supreme Court of the United States in 1877,[31] held that a Michigan statute that established rules for solemnization of marriages did not abolish pre-existing common-law marriage, because the statute did not affirmatively require statutory solemnization and was silent as to preexisting common law.

In almost all areas of the law (even those where there is a statutory framework, such as contracts for the sale of goods,[32] or the criminal law),[33] legislature-enacted statutes generally give only terse statements of general principle, and the fine boundaries and definitions exist only in the common law (connotation 1). To find out what the precise law is that applies to a particular set of facts, one has to locate precedential decisions on the topic, and reason from those decisions by analogy. To consider but one example, the First Amendment to the United States Constitution states "Congress shall make no law respecting an establishment of religion, or prohibiting the free exercise thereof"—but interpretation (that is, determining the fine boundaries, and resolving the tension between the "establishment" and "free exercise" clauses) of each of the important terms was delegated by Article III of the Constitution to the judicial branch,[34] so that the current legal boundaries of the Constitutional text can only be determined by consulting the common law.[35]

In common law jurisdictions, legislatures operate under the assumption that statutes will be interpreted against the backdrop of the pre-existing common law and custom. For example, in most U.S. states, the criminal statutes are primarily codification of pre-existing common law. (Codification is the process of enacting a statute that collects and restates pre-existing law in a single document—when that pre-existing law is common law, the common law remains relevant to the interpretation of these statutes.) In reliance on this assumption, modern statutes often leave a number of terms and fine distinctions unstated—for example, a statute might be very brief, leaving the precise definition of terms unstated, under the assumption that these fine distinctions will be inherited from pre-existing common law. (For this reason, many modern American law schools teach the common law of crime as it stood in England in 1789, because that centuries-old English common law is a necessary foundation to interpreting modern criminal statutes.)

With the transition from English law, which had common law crimes, to the new legal system under the U.S. Constitution, which prohibited *ex post facto* laws at both the federal and state level, the question was raised whether there could be common law crimes in the United States. It was settled in the case of *United States v. Hudson and Goodwin*, 11 U.S. 32 [36] (1812), which decided that federal courts had no jurisdiction to define new common law crimes, and that there must always be a (constitutional) statute defining the offense and the penalty for it.

Still, many states retain selected common law crimes. For example, in Virginia, the definition of the conduct that constitutes the crime of robbery exists only in the common law, and the robbery statute only sets the punishment.[37] Virginia Code section 1-200 establishes the continued existence and vitality of common law principles and provides that "The common law of England, insofar as it is not repugnant to the principles of the Bill of Rights and Constitution of this Commonwealth, shall continue in full force within the same, and be the rule of decision, except as altered by the General Assembly."

By contrast to statutory codification of common law, some statutes displace common law, for example to create a new cause of action that did not exist in the common law, or to legislatively overrule the common law. An example is the tort of wrongful death, which allows certain persons, usually a spouse, child or estate, to sue for damages on behalf of the deceased. There is no such tort in English common law; thus, any jurisdiction that lacks a wrongful death statute will not allow a lawsuit for the wrongful death of a loved one. Where a wrongful death statute exists, the compensation or other remedy available is limited to the remedy specified in the statute (typically, an upper limit on the amount of damages). Courts generally interpret statutes that create new causes of action narrowly – that is, limited to their precise terms—because the courts generally recognize the legislature as being supreme in deciding the reach of judge-made law unless such statute should violate some "second order" constitutional law provision (*cf.* judicial activism).

Where a tort is rooted in common law, all traditionally recognized damages for that tort may be sued for, whether or not there is mention of those damages in the current statutory law. For instance, a person who sustains bodily injury through the negligence of another may sue for medical costs, pain, suffering, loss of earnings or earning capacity, mental and/or emotional distress, loss of quality of life, disfigurement and more. These damages need not be set forth in statute as they already exist in the tradition of common law. However, without a wrongful death statute, most of them are extinguished upon death.

In the United States, the power of the federal judiciary to review and invalidate unconstitutional acts of the federal executive branch is stated in the constitution, Article III sections 1 and 2: "The judicial Power of the United States, shall be vested in one supreme Court, and in such inferior Courts as the Congress may from time to time ordain and establish. ... The judicial Power shall extend to all Cases, in Law and Equity, arising under this Constitution, the Laws of the United States, and Treaties made, or which shall be made, under their Authority..." The first famous statement of "the judicial power" was *Marbury v. Madison*, 5 U.S. (1 Cranch) 137 [38] (1803). Later cases interpreted the "judicial power" of Article III to establish the power of federal courts to consider or overturn any action of Congress or of any state that conflicts with the Constitution.

Overruling precedent—the limits of *stare decisis*

The United States federal courts are divided into twelve regional circuits, each with a circuit court of appeals (plus a thirteenth, the Court of Appeals for the Federal Circuit, which hears appeals in patent cases and cases against the federal government, without geographic limitation). Decisions of one circuit court are binding on the district courts within the circuit and on the circuit court itself, but are only persuasive authority on sister circuits. District court decisions are not binding precedent at all, only persuasive.

Most of the U.S. federal courts of appeal have adopted a rule under which, in the event of any conflict in decisions of panels (most of the courts of appeal almost always sit in panels of three), the earlier panel decision is controlling, and a panel decision may only be overruled by the court of appeals sitting *en banc* (that is, all active judges of the court) or by a higher court.[39] In these courts, the older decision remains controlling when an issue comes up the third time.

Other courts, for example, the Court of Customs and Patent Appeals and the Supreme Court, always sit *en banc*, and thus the *later* decision controls. These courts essentially overrule all previous cases in each new case, and older cases survive only to the extent they do not conflict with newer cases. The interpretations of these courts - for example, Supreme Court interpretations of the constitution or federal statutes - are stable only so long as the older interpretation maintains the support of a majority of the court. Older decisions persist through some combination of belief that the old decision is right, and that it is not sufficiently wrong to be overruled.

In the UK, since 2009, the Supreme Court of the United Kingdom has the authority to overrule and unify decisions of lower courts. From 1966 to 2009, this power lay with the House of Lords, granted by the Practice Statement of 1966.[40]

Canada's system, described below, avoids regional variability of federal law by giving national jurisdiction to both layers of appellate courts.

Common law as a foundation for commercial economies

The reliance on judicial opinion is a strength of common law systems, and is a significant contributor to the robust commercial systems in the United Kingdom and United States. Because there is reasonably precise guidance on almost every issue, parties (especially commercial parties) can predict whether a proposed course of action is likely to be lawful or unlawful. This ability to predict gives more freedom to come close to the boundaries of the law.[41] For example, many commercial contracts are more economically efficient, and create greater wealth, because the parties know ahead of time that the proposed arrangement, though perhaps close to the line, is almost certainly legal. Newspapers, taxpayer-funded entities with some religious affiliation, and political parties can obtain fairly clear guidance on the boundaries within which their freedom of expression rights apply.

In contrast, in non-common-law countries, and jurisdictions with very weak respect for precedent (example, the U.S. Patent Office), fine questions of law are redetermined anew each time they arise, making consistency and prediction more difficult, and procedures far more protracted than necessary because parties cannot rely on written statements of law as reliable guides. In jurisdictions that do not have a strong allegiance to a large body of precedent, parties have less *a priori* guidance and must often leave a bigger "safety margin" of unexploited opportunities, and final determinations are reached only after far larger expenditures on legal fees by the parties.

This is the reason for the frequent choice of the law of the State of New York in commercial contracts.[42] Commercial contracts almost always include a "choice of law clause" to reduce uncertainty. Somewhat surprisingly, contracts throughout the world (for example, contracts involving parties in Japan, France and Germany, and from most of the other states of the United States) often choose the law of New York, even where the relationship of the parties and transaction to New York is quite attenuated. Because of its history as the nation's commercial center, New York common law has a depth and predictability not (yet) available in any other jurisdiction. Similarly, corporations are often formed under Delaware corporate law, and contracts relating to corporate law issues (merger and acquisitions of companies, rights of shareholders, and so on.) include a Delaware choice of law clause, because of the deep body of law in Delaware on these issues.[43] On the other hand, some other jurisdictions have sufficiently developed bodies of law so that parties have no real motivation to choose the law of a foreign jurisdiction (for example, England and Wales, and the state of California), but not yet so fully developed that parties with no relationship to the jurisdiction choose that law.[44] The common theme in each case is that commercial parties seek predictability and simplicity in their contractual relations, and frequently choose the law of a common law jurisdiction with a well-developed body of common law to achieve that result.

Likewise, for litigation of commercial disputes arising out of unpredictable torts (as opposed to the prospective choice of law clauses in contracts discussed in the previous paragraph), certain jurisdictions attract an unusually high fraction of cases, because of the predictability afforded by the depth of decided cases. For example, London is considered the pre-eminent centre for litigation of admiralty cases.[45]

This is not to say that common law is better in every situation. For example, civil law can be clearer than case law when the legislature has had the foresight and diligence to address the precise set of facts applicable to a particular situation. For that reason, civil law statutes tend to be somewhat more detailed than statutes written by common law legislatures – but, conversely, that tends to make the statute more difficult to read (the United States tax code is an example).[46] Nonetheless, as a practical matter, no civil law legislature can ever address the full spectrum of factual possibilities in the breadth, depth and detail of the case law of the common law courts of even a smaller jurisdiction, and that deeper, more complete body of law provides additional predictability that promotes commerce.

History

The term "common law" originally derives from the 1150s and 1160s, when Henry II of England established the secular English tribunals. The "common law" was the law that emerged as "common" throughout the realm (as distinct from the various legal codes that preceded it, such as Mercian law, the Danelaw and the law of Wessex)[47] as the king's judges followed each other's decisions to create a unified common law throughout England. The doctrine of precedent developed during the 12th and 13th centuries,[48] as the collective judicial decisions that were based in tradition, custom and precedent.[49]

The form of reasoning used in common law is known as casuistry or case-based reasoning. The common law, as applied in civil cases (as distinct from criminal cases), was devised as a means of compensating someone for wrongful acts known as torts, including both intentional torts and torts caused by negligence, and as developing the body of law recognizing and regulating contracts. The type of procedure practiced in common law courts is known as the adversarial system; this is also a development of the common law.

Medieval English common law

In the late 800s, Alfred the Great assembled the Doom book (not to be confused with the more-famous Domesday Book from 200 years later), which collected the existing laws of Kent, Wessex, and Mercia, and attempted to blend in the Mosaic code, Christian principles, and Germanic customs dating as far as the fifth century.[50]

Before the Norman conquest in 1066, justice was administered primarily by what is today known as the county courts (the modern "counties" were referred to as "Shires" in pre-Norman times), presided by the diocesan bishop and the sheriff, exercising both ecclesiastical and civil jurisdiction.[51] Trial by jury began in these courts.[51]

In 1154, Henry II became the first Plantagenet king. Among many achievements, Henry institutionalized common law by creating a unified system of law "common" to the country through incorporating and elevating local custom to the national, ending local control and peculiarities, eliminating arbitrary remedies and reinstating a jury system – citizens sworn on oath to investigate reliable criminal accusations and civil claims. The jury reached its verdict through evaluating common local knowledge, not necessarily through the presentation of evidence, a distinguishing factor from today's civil and criminal court systems.

Henry II developed the practice of sending judges from his own central court to hear the various disputes throughout the country. His judges would resolve disputes on an ad hoc basis according to what they interpreted the customs to be. The king's judges would then return to London and often discuss their cases and the decisions they made with the other judges. These decisions would be recorded and filed. In time, a rule, known as *stare decisis* (also commonly known as precedent) developed, whereby a judge would be bound to follow the decision of an earlier judge; he was required to adopt the earlier judge's interpretation of the law and apply the same principles promulgated by that earlier judge if the two cases had similar facts to one another. Once judges began to regard each other's decisions to be binding precedent, the pre-Norman system of local customs and law varying in each locality was replaced by a system that was (at least in theory, though not always in practice) common throughout the whole country, hence the name "common law."

Henry II's creation of a powerful and unified court system, which curbed somewhat the power of canonical (church) courts, brought him (and England) into conflict with the church, most famously with Thomas Becket, the Archbishop of Canterbury. Eventually, Becket was murdered inside Canterbury Cathedral by four knights who believed themselves to be acting on Henry's behalf. Whether Henry actually intended to bring about the assassination of Becket is debatable, but there is no question that at the time of the murder, the two men were embroiled in a bitter dispute regarding the power of Royal Courts to exercise jurisdiction over former clergymen. The murder of the Archbishop gave rise to a wave of popular outrage against the King. Henry was forced to repeal the disputed laws and to abandon his efforts to hold church members accountable for secular crimes (see also Constitutions of Clarendon).

Judge-made common law operated as the primary source of law for several hundred years, before Parliament acquired legislative powers to create statutory law. It is important to understand that common law is the older and more traditional source of law, and legislative power is simply a layer applied on top of the older common law foundation. Since the 12th century, courts have had parallel and co-equal authority to make law[52] -- "legislating from the bench" is a traditional and essential function of courts, which was carried over into the U.S. system as an essential component of the "judicial power" specified by Article III of the U.S. constitution.[53] Justice Oliver Wendell Holmes, Jr. observed in 1917 that "judges do and must legislate."[54] There are legitimate debates on how the powers of courts and legislatures should be balanced. However, a view that courts lack law-making power is historically inaccurate and constitutionally unsupportable.

Influences of foreign legal systems

Roman law

The term "common law" (connotation 2) is often used as a contrast to Roman-derived "civil law", and the fundamental processes and forms of reasoning in the two are quite different. Nonetheless, there has been considerable cross-fertilization of ideas, while the two traditions and sets of foundational principles remain distinct.

By the time of the rediscovery of the Roman law in Europe in the 12th and 13th centuries, the common law had already developed far enough to prevent a Roman law reception as it occurred on the continent.[55] However, the first common law scholars, most notably Glanvill and Bracton, as well as the early royal common law judges, had been well accustomed with Roman law. Often, they were clerics trained in the Roman canon law.[56] One of the first and throughout its history one of the most significant treatises of the common law, Bracton's *De Legibus et Consuetudinibus Angliae* (On the Laws and Customs of England), was heavily influenced by the division of the law in Justinian's *Institutes*.[57] The impact Roman law had decreased sharply after the age of Bracton, but the Roman divisions of actions into *in rem* (typically, actions against a *thing* or property for the purpose of gaining title to that property; must be filed in a court where the property is located) and *in personam* (typically, actions directed against a person; these can affect a person's rights and, since a person often owns things, his property too) used by Bracton had a lasting effect and laid the groundwork for a return of Roman law structural concepts in the 18th and 19th centuries. Signs of this can be found in Blackstone's *Commentaries on the Laws of England*,[58] and Roman law ideas regained importance with the revival of academic law schools in the 19th century.[59] As a result, today, the main systematic divisions of the law into property, contract, and tort (and to some extent unjust enrichment) can be found in the civil law as well as in the common law.[60]

Propagation of the common law to the colonies and Commonwealth by reception statutes

Initial reception of English common law into new colonies, and adoption of common law on decolonization

In *Commentaries on the Laws of England* (Bk I, ch.4, pp 106–108), Sir William Blackstone described the process by which English common law followed English colonization:

> Plantations or colonies, in distant countries, are either such where the lands are claimed by right of occupancy only, by finding them desert and uncultivated, and peopling them from the mother-country; or where, when already cultivated, they have been either gained by conquest, or ceded to us by treaties. And both these rights are founded upon the law of nature, or at least upon that of nations. But there is a difference between these two species of colonies, with respect to the laws by which they are bound. For it hath been held, that if an uninhabited country be discovered and planted by English subjects, all the English laws then in being, which are the birthright of every subject, are immediately there in force... But in conquered or ceded countries, that have already laws of their own, the king may indeed alter and change those laws; but, till he does actually change them, the ancient laws of the country remain, unless such as are against the law of God, as in the case of an infidel country.

In other words, if an 'uninhabited' or 'infidel' territory is colonized by Britain, then the English law automatically applies in this territory from the moment of colonization; however if the colonized territory has a pre-existing legal system, the native law would apply (effectively a form of indirect rule) until formally superseded by the English law, through Royal Prerogative subjected to the Westminster Parliament.

As colonies gained independence from Britain, in most cases the newly independent countries adopted English common law precedent as of the date of independence as the default law to carry forward into the new nation, to the extent not explicitly rejected by the newly freed colony's founding documents or government. In some cases, the carry-forward was simply understood, with no express provision in either the new independence constitution or legislation. In other cases, the new legislature felt it necessary to "dot i's and cross t's" by enacting an express reception statute, even if common law had been received during the colonial period. Examples of both patterns are described below.

Reception statutes in the United States

For example, following the American Revolution in 1776, one of the first legislative acts undertaken by each of the newly independent states was to adopt a "reception statute" that gave legal effect to the existing body of English common law to the extent that American legislation or the Constitution had not explicitly rejected English law.[61] Some states enacted reception statutes as legislative statutes, while other states received the English common law through provisions of the state's constitution, and some by court decision. British traditions such as the monarchy were rejected by the U.S. Constitution, but many English common law traditions such as habeas corpus, jury trials, and various other civil liberties were adopted in the United States. Significant elements of English common law prior to 1776 still remain in effect in many jurisdictions in the United States, because they have never been rejected by American courts or legislatures.[62]

For example, the New York Constitution of 1777[63] provides that:

> [S]uch parts of the common law of England, and of the statute law of England and Great Britain, and of the acts of the legislature of the colony of New York, as together did form the law of the said colony on the 19th day of April, in the year of our Lord one thousand seven hundred and seventy-five, shall be and continue the law of this State, subject to such alterations and provisions as the legislature of this State shall, from time to time, make concerning the same.

Alexander Hamilton emphasized in The Federalist that this New York constitutional provision expressly made the common law subject "to such alterations and provisions as the legislature shall from time to time make concerning the same."[64] Thus, even when reception was effected by a constitution, the common law was still subject to alteration by a legislature's statute.

One could note a certain irony: one of the first acts of many of the newly independent states was to adopt the law of the foreign sovereign from whom independence had just been gained. But this is one more demonstration of the point mentioned above (Commercial economies), that the newly independent states recognized the importance of a predictable and established body of law to govern the conduct of citizens and businesses, and therefore adopted the richest available source of law.

The Northwest Ordinance, which was approved by the Congress of the Confederation in 1787, guaranteed "judicial proceedings according to the course of the common law." Nathan Dane, the primary author of the Northwest Ordinance, viewed this provision as a default mechanism in the event that federal or territorial statutes were silent about a particular matter; he wrote that if "a statute makes an offence, and is silent as to the mode of trial, it shall be by jury, according to the course of the common law."[65] In effect, the provision operated as a reception statute, giving legal authority to the established common law in the vast territories where no states had yet been established.

Over time, as new states were formed from federal territories, these territorial reception statutes became obsolete and were re-enacted as state law. For example, a reception statute enacted by legislation in the state of Washington requires that "[t]he common law, so far as it is not inconsistent with the Constitution and laws of the United States, or of the state of Washington nor incompatible with the institutions and condition of society in this state, shall be the rule of decision in all the courts of this state."[66] In this way, the common law was eventually incorporated into the legal systems of every state except Louisiana (which inherited a civil law system from its French colonizers before the Louisiana Purchase of 1803, adopting a code similar to but not directly based on the Napoleonic Code of 1804).

Reception in Canada

The Canadian colonies received the common law and English statutes under Blackstone's principles for the establishment of the legal system of a new colony. In five of the Canadian provinces, English law was received automatically, under the principle of a settled colony inheriting English law. In the other five provinces and the three territories, reception was governed by reception statutes. The reception of English law occurred long before Canada became fully independent, and reception statutes in Canada were not part of the decolonisation process.

When Canada achieved formal independence with the passage of the Canada Act 1982, no reception statutes were necessary for the decolonialisation process. English law had already been received in the various Canadian provinces and territories by legislation and judicial decisions over the previous two centuries.

Atlantic Provinces

In the four Atlantic provinces (Nova Scotia, New Brunswick, Prince Edward Island, and Newfoundland and Labrador), the reception of English law was automatic, under the principle set out by Blackstone relating to settled colonies. British colonists were considered to have brought English common law as well as applicable English statutes with them. No reception statute was necessary. The reception date for New Brunswick is 1660; for Nova Scotia and Prince Edward Island, 1758; and for Newfoundland and Labrador, 1825.

Quebec

Quebec was settled as a French colony, and originally operated under the French civil law system, using the *coûtume de Paris*. Upon the transfer of the colony to British control, the British government issued the Royal Proclamation of 1763, which imposed English common law on the colony, under the principle set out in Blackstone relating to captured colonies. However, in 1774, the British Parliament passed the Quebec Act, which restored the French civil law for matters of private law (e.g., contracts, property, successions), while keeping the English common law as the basis for public law in the colony, notably the criminal law. Subsequently, with the passage of the Civil Code of Lower Canada in 1866, Quebec's civil law became entirely statute based, using the civil law system for matters within provincial jurisdiction. Public law in Quebec continues to have its origin in the common law, but even here civil law plays a strong role. Where federal legislation requires interpretation, judges must look to the Civil Code of Quebec.[67]

Ontario

The territory now forming Ontario was originally part of Quebec, and thus was under the civil law. When Quebec was divided into the two provinces of Upper and Lower Canada by the Constitutional Act of 1791, the first Act passed by the Legislature of Upper Canada was to adopt the law of England for all purposes, replacing the civil law.[68] This statute adopted both the English common law and English statute law. The foundation for the operation of the common law in Ontario traces back to that reception statute.

The North-West Territories, Manitoba, Saskatchewan and Alberta

The new Dominion of Canada acquired the territories of Rupert's Land and the North-Western Territory from the Hudson's Bay Company in 1870. These territories were considered to have been settled by British colonists, and therefore the reception of English law was automatic. However, given the long history of control by the Hudson's Bay Company, there was some uncertainty as to the date of reception. To resolve this uncertainty, various statutes were passed to set the date of reception as July 15, 1870, the date of the transfer of these two territories to Canada.

The Province of Manitoba set this date for the reception of English law for matters coming within provincial jurisdiction. The Legislature of the North-West Territories passed an Ordinance adopting the same date for matters coming within territorial jurisdiction. The federal Parliament eventually enacted a provision adopting this date for all matters in the North-West Territories.[69] That provision was carried forward in the provinces of Alberta and Saskatchewan, when they were created by the Alberta Act[70] and the Saskatchewan Act.[71] The same provision is the basis for the reception date of English law in the Northwest Territories, Yukon and Nunavut.

British Columbia

British Columbia was considered to be a settled colony and therefore received English law automatically, under the principle set out by Blackstone.

Reception in Hong Kong

When Hong Kong was handed over to China in 1997, Hong Kong retained the common law through a reception statute in Chapter I, Article 8 of the Hong Kong Basic Law:[72]

> The laws previously in force in Hong Kong, that is, the common law, rules of equity, ordinances, subordinate legislation and customary law shall be maintained, except for any that contravene this Law, and subject to any amendment by the legislature of the Hong Kong Special Administrative Region.

Reception in other British colonies

The pattern was repeated in many other former British colonies as they gained independence from the United Kingdom. Ireland, Australia, New Zealand, India, Belize, and various Caribbean and African nations have adopted English common law through reception statutes although they do not inevitably continue to copy English Common Law; later cases can often draw on decisions in other Common Law jurisdictions.

Decline of Latin maxims, and adding flexibility to *stare decisis*

Well into the 19th century, ancient maxims played a large role in common law adjudication. Many of these maxims had originated in Roman Law, migrated to England before the introduction of Christianity to the British Isles, and were typically stated in Latin even in English decisions. Many examples are familiar in everyday speech even today, "One cannot be a judge in one's own cause" (see Dr. Bonham's Case), rights are reciprocal to obligations, and the like. Judicial decisions and treatises of the 17th and 18th centuries, such at those of Lord Chief Justice Edward Coke, presented the common law as a collection of such maxims. See also Thomas Jefferson's letter to Thomas Cooper.

Reliance on old maxims and rigid adherence to precedent, no matter how old or ill-considered, was under full attack by the late 19th century. Oliver Wendell Holmes, Jr. in his famous article, "The Path of the Law",[73] commented, "It is revolting to have no better reason for a rule of law than that so it was laid down in the time of Henry IV. It is still more revolting if the grounds upon which it was laid down have vanished long since, and the rule simply persists from blind imitation of the past." Justice Holmes noted that study of maxims might be sufficient for "the man of the present," but "the man of the future is the man of statistics and the master of economics." In an 1880 lecture at Harvard, he wrote:

> The life of the law has not been logic; it has been experience. The felt necessities of the time, the prevalent moral and political theories, intuitions of public policy, avowed or unconscious, even the prejudices which judges share with their fellow men, have had a good deal more to do than the syllogism in determining the rules by which men should be governed. The law embodies the story of a nation's development through many centuries, and it cannot be dealt with as if it contained only the axioms and corollaries of a book of mathematics.

In the early 20th century, Louis Brandeis, later appointed to the United States Supreme Court, became noted for his use of policy-driving facts and economics in his briefs, and extensive appendices presenting facts that lead a judge to the advocate's conclusion. By this time, briefs relied more on facts than on Latin maxims.

Reliance on old maxims is now deprecated.[74] Common law decisions today reflect both precedent and policy judgment drawn from economics, the social sciences, business, decisions of foreign courts, and the like. The degree to which these external factors *should* influence adjudication is the subject of active debate, but that judges *do* draw of learning from other fields and jurisdictions is a fact of modern legal life.

1870 through 20th century, and the procedural merger of law and equity

As early as the 15th century, it became the practice that litigants who felt they had been cheated by the common-law system would petition the King in person. For example, they might argue that an award of damages (at common law) was not sufficient redress for a trespasser occupying their land, and instead request that the trespasser be evicted. From this developed the system of equity, administered by the Lord Chancellor, in the courts of chancery. By their nature, equity and law were frequently in conflict and litigation would frequently continue for years as one court countermanded the other,[75] even though it was established by the 17th century that equity should prevail. A famous example is the fictional case of Jarndyce and Jarndyce in *Bleak House*, by Charles Dickens.[76]

In England, courts of law and equity were combined by the Judicature Acts of 1873 and 1875, with equity being supreme in case of conflict.[76]

In the United States, parallel systems of law (providing money damages, with cases heard by a jury upon either party's request) and equity (fashioning a remedy to fit the situation, including injunctive relief, heard by a judge) survived well into the 20th century. The United States federal courts procedurally separated law and equity: the same judges could hear either kind of case, but a given case could only pursue causes in law or in equity, and the two kinds of cases proceeded under different procedural rules. This became problematic when a given case required both money damages and injunctive relief. In 1937, the new Federal Rules of Civil Procedure combined law and equity into one form of action, the "civil action." Fed.R.Civ.P. 2. The distinction survives to the extent that issues that were "common law" as of 1791 (the date of adoption of the Seventh Amendment) are still subject to the right of either party to request a jury, and "equity" issues are decided by a judge.[77]

Alabama, Delaware, Mississippi, New Jersey, Tennessee still have separate courts of law and equity, for example, the Court of Chancery. In many states there are separate divisions for law and equity within one court.

Common law pleading and its abolition in the early 20th century

For centuries, through the 19th century, the common law recognized only specific forms of action, and required very careful drafting of the opening pleading (called a writ) to slot into one of them: Debt, Detinue, Covenant, Special Assumpsit, General Assumpsit, Trespass, Trover, Replevin, Case (or Trespass on the Case), and Ejectment.[78] To initiate a law suit, a pleading had to be drafted to meet myriad technical requirements: correctly categorizing the case into the correct legal pigeonhole (pleading in the alternative was not permitted), and using specific "magic words" encrusted over the centuries. Under the old common law pleading standards, a suit by a *pro se* ("for oneself," without a lawyer) party was all but impossible, and there was often considerable procedural jousting at the outset of a case over minor wording issues.

One of the major reforms of the late 19th century and early 20th century was the abolition of common law pleading requirements.[79] A plaintiff can initiate a case by giving the defendant "a short and plain statement" of facts that constitute an alleged wrong. This reform moved the attention of courts from technical scrutiny of words to a more rational consideration of the facts, and opened access to justice far more broadly.

Contrasts between common law and civil law systems

Adversarial system vs. inquisitorial system

Common law courts tend to use an adversarial system, in which two sides present their cases to a neutral judge. In contrast, in civil law systems, inquisitorial system proceedings, where an examining magistrate serves two roles by developing the evidence and arguments for one and the other side during the investigation phase.

The examining magistrate then presents the dossier detailing his or her findings to the president of the bench that will adjudicate on the case where it has been decided that a trial shall be conducted. Therefore the president of the bench's view of the case is not neutral and may be biased while conducting the trial after the reading of the dossier. Unlike the common law proceedings, the president of the bench in the inquisitorial system is not merely an umpire and is entitled to directly interview the witnesses or express comments during the trial, as long as he or she does not express his or her view on the guilt of the accused.

The proceeding in the inquisitorial system is essentially by writing. Most of the witnesses would have given evidence in the investigation phase and such evidence will be contained in the dossier under the form of police reports. In the same way, the accused would have already put his or her case at the investigation phase but he or she will be free to change her or his evidence at trial. Whether the accused pleads guilty or not, a trial will be conducted. Unlike the adversarial system, the conviction and sentence to be served (if any) will be released by the trial jury together with the president of the trial bench, following their common deliberation.

There are many exceptions in both directions. For example, most proceedings before U.S. federal and state agencies are inquisitorial in nature, at least the initial stages (*e.g.*, a patent examiner, a social security hearing officer, and so on.) even though the law to be applied is developed through common law processes.

Contrasting role of treatises and academic writings in common law and civil law systems

The role of the legal academy presents a significant "cultural" difference between common law (connotation 2) and civil law jurisdictions.

In common law jurisdictions, legal treatises compile common law decisions, and state overarching principles that (in the author's opinion) explain the results of the cases. However, in common law jurisdictions, treatises are not the law, and lawyers and judges tend to use these treatises as only "finding aids" to locate the relevant cases. In common law jurisdictions, scholarly work is seldom cited as authority for what the law is.[80] When common law courts rely on scholarly work, it is almost always only for factual findings, policy justification, or the history and evolution of the law, but the court's legal conclusion is reached through analysis of relevant statutes and common law, seldom scholarly commentary.

In contrast, in civil law jurisdictions, the writings of law professors are given significant weight by courts. In part, this is because civil law decisions traditionally were very brief, sometimes no more than a paragraph stating who wins and who loses. The rationale has to come from somewhere else, and the academy often filled that role. As civil law court decisions move in the direction of common law reasoning, it is possible that this balance may shift.

Common law legal systems in the present day

Civil law

Common law

Bijuridical (Civil and Common law)

Islamic law

Legal systems of the world.

The common law constitutes the basis of the legal systems of: England and Wales, Northern Ireland, Ireland, federal law in the United States and the law of individual U.S. states (except Louisiana), federal law throughout Canada and the law of the individual provinces and territories (except Quebec), Australia (both federal and individual states), Kenya, New Zealand, South Africa, India,Myanmar,[9] Malaysia, Bangladesh, Brunei, Pakistan, Singapore, Hong Kong, Antigua and Barbuda, Barbados, The Bahamas, Belize, Dominica, Grenada, Jamaica, St. Vincent and the Granadines, Saint Kitts and Nevis, Trinidad and Tobago, and many other generally English-speaking countries or Commonwealth countries (except Scotland, which is bijuridicial, and Malta). Essentially, every country that was colonised at some time by England, Great Britain, or the United Kingdom uses common law except those that were formerly colonised by other nations, such as Quebec (which follows the law of France in part), South Africa and Sri Lanka (which follow Roman Dutch law), where the prior civil law system was retained to respect the civil rights of the local colonists. India uses common law except in the state of Goa which retains the Portuguese civil code. Guyana and Saint Lucia have mixed Common Law and Civil Law systems.

Scotland

Scotland is often said to use the civil law system but it has a unique system that combines elements of an uncodified civil law dating back to the Corpus Juris Civilis with an element of common law long predating the Treaty of Union with England in 1707 (see Legal institutions of Scotland in the High Middle Ages). Scots common law differs in that the use of *precedents* is subject to the courts' seeking to discover the principle that justifies a law rather than searching for an example as a *precedent*, and principles of natural justice and fairness have always played a role in Scots Law. Comparable pluralistic (or 'mixed') legal systems operate in Quebec, Louisiana and South Africa.

States of the United States (1600s on)

New York (1600s)

The state of New York, which also has a civil law history from its Dutch colonial days, also began a codification of its law in the 19th century. The only part of this codification process that was considered complete is known as the Field Code applying to civil procedure. The original colony of New Netherlands was settled by the Dutch and the law was also Dutch. When the English captured pre-existing colonies they continued to allow the local settlers to keep their civil law. However, the Dutch settlers revolted against the English and the colony was recaptured by the Dutch. When the English finally regained control of New Netherland they forced, as a punishment unique in the history of the British Empire, the English common law upon all the colonists, including the Dutch. This was problematic, as the patroon system of land holding, based on the feudal system and civil law, continued to operate in the colony until it was abolished in the mid-19th century. The influence of Roman Dutch law continued in the colony well into the late 19th century. The codification of a law of general obligations shows how remnants of the civil law tradition in New York continued on from the Dutch days.

Louisiana (1700s)

Uniquely among U.S. states, Louisiana's codified system, the Louisiana Civil Code, is based on principles of law from continental Europe instead of common law. These principles derive ultimately from Roman law, transmitted through Spanish and French law, as the state's current territory intersects the area of North America colonized by Spain and by France. Contrary to popular belief, the Louisiana code does not directly derive from the Napoleonic Code, as the latter was enacted in 1804, one year after the Louisiana Purchase. However, the two codes are similar in many respects due to common roots.

Historically notable among the Louisiana code's differences from common law is the role of property rights among women, particularly in inheritance gained by widows.

California (1850s)

The U.S. state of California has a system based on common law, but it has codified the law in the manner of the civil law jurisdictions. The reason for the enactment of the codes in California in the 19th century was to replace a pre-existing system based on Spanish civil law with a system based on common law, similar to that in most other states. California and a number of other Western states, however, have retained the concept of community property derived from civil law. The California courts have treated portions of the codes as an extension of the common-law tradition, subject to judicial development in the same manner as judge-made common law. (Most notably, in the case *Li v. Yellow Cab Co.*, 13 Cal.3d 804 (1975), the California Supreme Court adopted the principle of comparative negligence in the face of a California Civil Code provision codifying the traditional common-law doctrine of contributory negligence.)

United States federal system (1789 and 1938)

The United States federal government (as opposed to the states) has a variant on a common law system. United States federal courts only act as interpreters of statutes and the constitution by elaborating and precisely defining the broad language (connotation 1(b) above), but, unlike state courts, do not act as an independent source of common law (connotation 1(a) above).

Before 1938, the federal courts, like almost all other common law courts, decided the law on any issue where the relevant legislature (either the U.S. Congress or state legislature, depending on the issue), had not acted, by looking to courts in the same system, that is, other federal courts, even on issues of state law, and even where there was no express grant of authority from Congress or the Constitution.

In 1938, the U.S. Supreme Court in *Erie Railroad Co. v. Tompkins* 304 U.S. 64, 78 [81] (1938), overruled earlier precedent,[82] and held "There is no federal general common law," thus confining the federal courts to act only as interpreters of law originating elsewhere. *E.g., Texas Industries v. Radcliff*, 451 U.S. 630 [83] (1981) (without an express grant of statutory authority, federal courts cannot create rules of intuitive justice, for example, a right to contribution from co-conspirators). Post-1938, federal courts deciding issues that arise under state law are required to defer to state court interpretations of state statutes, or reason what a state's highest court would rule if presented with the issue, or to certify the question to the state's highest court for resolution.

Later courts have limited *Erie* slightly, to create a few situations where United States federal courts are permitted to create federal common law rules without express statutory authority, for example, where a federal rule of decision is necessary to protect uniquely federal interests, such as foreign affairs, or financial instruments issued by the federal government. *See, e.g., Clearfield Trust Co. v. United States*, 318 U.S. 363 [84] (1943) (giving federal courts the authority to fashion common law rules with respect to issues of federal power, in this case negotiable instruments backed by the federal government); *see also International News Service v. Associated Press*, 248 U.S. 215 [85] (1918) (creating a cause of action for misappropriation of "hot news" that lacks any statutory grounding, but that is one of the handful of federal common law actions that survives today); *National Basketball Association v. Motorola, Inc.*, 105 F.3d 841, 843-44, 853 (2d Cir. 1997) (noting continued vitality of INS "hot news" tort under New York state law, but leaving open the question of whether it survives under federal law). Except on Constitutional issues, Congress is free to legislatively overrule federal courts' common law.[86]

India (19th century and 1948)

Indian Law is largely based on English common law because of the long period of British colonial influence during the period of the British Raj.

After the failed rebellion against the British in 1857, the British Parliament took over the reign of India from the British East India Company, and British India came under the direct rule of the Crown. The British Parliament passed the Government of India Act of 1858 to this effect, which set up the structure of British government in India. It established in England the office of the Secretary of State for India through whom the Parliament would exercise its rule, along with a Council of India to aid him. It also established the office of the Governor-General of India along with an Executive Council in India, which consisted of high officials of the British Government.

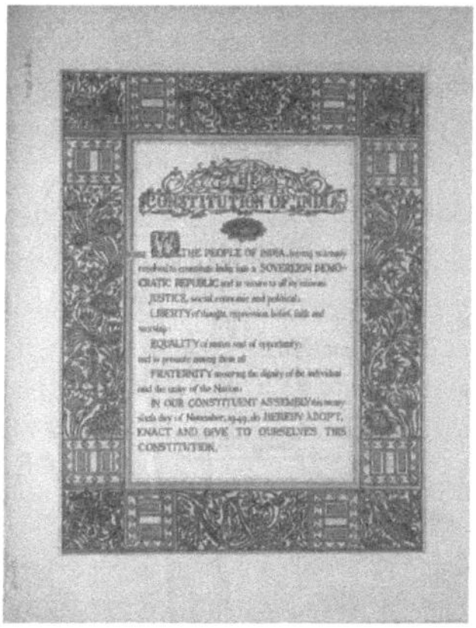

The Constitution of India is the longest written constitution for a country, containing 395 articles, 12 schedules, numerous amendments and 117,369 words.

Much of contemporary Indian law shows substantial European and American influence. Various legislations first introduced by the British are still in effect in their modified forms today. During the drafting of the Indian Constitution, laws from Ireland, the United States, Britain, and France were all synthesized to get a refined set of Indian laws, as it currently stands. Indian laws also adhere to the United Nations guidelines on human rights law and the environmental law. Certain international trade laws, such as those on intellectual property, are also enforced in India.

Indian family law is complex, with each religion adhering to its own specific laws. In most states, registering marriages and divorces is not compulsory. There are separate laws governing Hindus, Muslims, Christians, Sikhs and followers of other religions. The exception to this rule is in the state of Goa, where a Portuguese uniform civil code is in place, in which all religions have a common law regarding marriages, divorces and adoption.

Ancient India represented a distinct tradition of law, and had an historically independent school of legal theory and practice. The *Arthashastra*, dating from 400 BCE and the *Manusmriti*, from 100 CE, were influential treatises in India, texts that were considered authoritative legal guidance.[87] Manu's central philosophy was tolerance and pluralism, and was cited across Southeast Asia.[88] Early in this period, which finally culminated in the creation of the Gupta Empire, relations with ancient Greece and Rome were not infrequent. The appearance of similar fundamental institutions of international law in various parts of the world show that they are inherent in international society, irrespective of culture and tradition.[89] Inter-State relations in the pre-Islamic period resulted in clear-cut rules of warfare of a high humanitarian standard, in rules of neutrality, of treaty law, of customary law embodied in religious charters, in exchange of embassies of a temporary or semi-permanent character.[90] When India became part of the British Empire, there was a break in tradition, and Hindu and Islamic law were supplanted by the common law.[91] As a result, the present judicial system of the country derives largely from the British system and has little correlation to the institutions of the pre-British era.[92]

There are 1160 laws as on September 2007.[93]

Canada (1867)

All but one of the provinces of Canada use a common law system (the exception being Quebec, which uses a civil law system for issues arising within provincial jurisdiction, such as property ownership and contracts). Criminal law, which is uniform throughout Canada, is based on the common law as interpreted by the Supreme Court of Canada. The mid-tier Federal Court of Appeal is a single court that sits and hears cases in multiple cities, and thus mid-tier decisions have precedential value throughout Canada (that is, unlike the United States, Canada is not divided into appellate circuits).[94] Canadian federal statutes[95] must use the terminology of both the common law and civil law for those matters; this is referred to as legislative bijuralism.[96]

Nicaragua

Nicaragua's legal system also is a mixture of the English Common Law and the Civil Law through the influence of British administration of the Eastern half of the country from the mid-17th century until about 1905, the William Walker period from about 1855 through 1857, USA interventions/occupations during the period from 1909 to 1933, the influence of USA institutions during the Somoza family administrations (1933 through 1979) and the considerable importation between 1979 and the present of USA culture and institutions.

Israel (1948)

Israel has a mixed system of common law and civil law. While Israeli law is undergoing codification, its basic principles are inherited from the law of the British Mandate of Palestine and thus resemble those of British and American law, namely: the role of courts in creating the body of law and the authority of the supreme court in reviewing and if necessary overturning legislative and executive decisions, as well as employing the adversarial system. One of the primary reasons that the Israeli constitution remains unwritten is the fear by whatever party holds power that creating a written constitution, combined with the common-law elements, would severely limit the powers of the Knesset (which, following the doctrine of parliamentary sovereignty, holds near-unlimited power).[97]

Roman Dutch Common law

Roman Dutch Commons law is a bijuridical or mixed system of law similar to the common law system in Scotland and Louisiana. Roman Dutch common law jurisdictions include South Africa, Botswana, Lesotho, Namibia, Swaziland, Sri-Lanka and Zimbabwe. Many of these jurisdictions recognise customary law, and in some, such as South Africa the Constitution requires that the common law be developed in accordance with the Bill of Rights. Roman Dutch common law is a development of Roman Dutch law by courts in the Roman Dutch common law jurisdictions. During the Napoleonic wars the Kingdom of the Netherlands adopted the French *code civil* in 1809, however the Dutch colonies in the Cape of Good Hope and Sri Lanka, at the time called Ceylon, were seized by the British to prevent them being used as bases by the French Navy. The system was developed by the courts and spread with the expansion of British colonies in Southern Africa. Roman Dutch common law relies on legal principles set out in Roman law sources such as Justinian's Institutes and Digest, and also on the writing of Dutch jurists of the 15th century such as Grotius and Voet. In practice the majority of decisions rely on recent precedent.

Alternatives to common law systems

The main alternative to the common law system is the civil law system, which is used in Continental Europe, and most of the rest of the world. The contrast between civil law and common law legal systems has become increasingly blurred, with the growing importance of jurisprudence (similar to case law but not binding) in civil law countries, and the growing importance of statute law and codes in common law countries.

Examples of common law being replaced by statute or codified rule in the United States include criminal law (since 1812, U.S. courts have held that criminal law must be embodied in statute if the public is to have fair notice), commercial law (the Uniform Commercial Code in the early 1960s) and procedure (the Federal Rules of Civil Procedure in the 1930s and the Federal Rules of Evidence in the 1970s). But note that in each case, the statute sets the general principles, but the common law process determines the scope and application of the statute.

An example of convergence from the other direction is shown in Srl CILFIT and Lanificio di Gavardo SpA v Ministry of Health (Corte suprema di Cassazione, Italy, 1982) [98], in which Italy's Supreme Court held that questions it has already answered need not be resubmitted. This brought in a distinctly common law principle into an essentially civil law jurisdiction. The Italian courts continue to follow this precedent and assume that the Supreme Court's rulings have precedential value.

The former Soviet Bloc and other Socialist countries used a Socialist law system.

Much of the Muslim world uses Sharia (also called Islamic law).

Scholarly works

Lord Chief Justice Edward Coke, a 17th-century English jurist and Member of Parliament, wrote several legal texts that formed the basis for the modern common law, with lawyers in both England and America learning their law from his *Institutes* and *Reports* until the end of the 18th century. His works are still cited by common law courts around the world.

Sir William Blackstone as illustrated in his *Commentaries on the Laws of England.*

The next definitive historical treatise on the common law is *Commentaries on the Laws of England,* written by Sir William Blackstone and first published in 1765–1769. Since 1979, a facsimile edition of that first edition has been available in four paper-bound volumes. Today it has been superseded in the English part of the United Kingdom by Halsbury's Laws of England that covers both common and statutory English law.

While he was still on the Massachusetts Supreme Judicial Court, and before being named to the U.S. Supreme Court, Justice Oliver Wendell Holmes, Jr. published a short volume called *The Common Law*, which remains a classic in the field. Unlike Blackstone and the Restatements, Holmes' book only briefly discusses what the law *is*; rather, Holmes describes the common law *process*. Law professor John Chipman Gray's *The Nature and Sources of the Law*, an examination and survey of the common law, is also still commonly read in U.S. law schools.

In the United States, Restatements of various subject matter areas (Contracts, Torts, Judgments, and so on.), edited by the American Law Institute, collect the common law for the area. The ALI Restatements are often cited by American courts and lawyers for propositions of uncodified common law, and are considered highly persuasive authority, just below binding precedential decisions. The Corpus Juris Secundum is an encyclopedia whose main content is a compendium of the common law and its variations throughout the various state jurisdictions.

Scots *common law* covers matters including murder and theft, and has sources in custom, in legal writings and previous court decisions. The legal writings used are called *Institutional Texts* and come mostly from the 17th, 18th and 19th centuries. Examples include Craig, *Jus Feudale* (1655) and Stair, *The Institutions of the Law of Scotland* (1681).

See also

- Anglo-Saxon law
- Common law offences
- Alimony
- Doom book, or Code of Alfred the Great
- Arraignment
- Civil law (legal system)
- Common-law marriage
- Russian law
- English law
- Grand jury
- Jury trial

References

[1] Duhaime's Law Dictionary, "Definition of Common Law" (http://www.duhaime.org/LegalDictionary/C/CommonLaw.aspx)
[2] Washington Probate, "Estate Planning & Probate Glossary", *Washington (State) Probate*, s.v. "common law", [htm], 8 Dec. 2008: <http://www.wa-probate.com/Intro/Estate-Probate-Glossary.htm>, retrieved on 7 November 2009.
[3] Charles Arnold-Baker, *The Companion to British History*, s.v. "English Law" (London: Loncross Denholm Press, 2008), 484.
[4] *Marbury v. Madison*, 5 U.S. 137 (http://caselaw.lp.findlaw.com/scripts/getcase.pl?navby=CASE&court=US&vol=5&page=137) (1803) ("It is emphatically the province and duty of the judicial department to say what the law is. Those who apply the rule to particular cases, must of necessity expound and interpret that rule. If two laws conflict with each other, the courts must decide on the operation of each.")
[5] http://www.britannica.com/EBchecked/topic/188090/English-law ; British History: Middle Ages "Common Law – Henry II and the Birth of a State" (http://www.bbc.co.uk/history/british/middle_ages/henryii_law_01.shtml). BBC. . Retrieved 2009-07-23.
[6] K. G. Balakrishnan (23–24 March 2008). *An Overview of the Indian Justice Delivery Mechanism* (http://www.supremecourtofindia.nic.in/speeches/speeches_2008/abu_dhabi__as_delivered.pdf) (Speech). International Conference of the Presidents of the Supreme Courts of the World. Abu Dhabi. . Retrieved 1 August 2012. "India, being a common law country, derives most of its modern judicial framework from the British legal system."
[7] "...."*in a common law jurisdiction such as ours*"" (http://www.supremecourt.gov.pk/web/user_files/File/REVIEW_P_46&47_2011_full.pdf) (PDF). . Retrieved 2012-02-22.
[8] "The Common Law in the World: the Australian Experience" (http://w3.uniroma1.it/idc/centro/publications/43finn.pdf). W3.uniroma1.it. . Retrieved 2010-05-30.
[9] http://en.wikipedia.org/wiki/Politics_of_Burma
[10] "Parliament of Barbados: one of the oldest Constitutions in the Commonwealth" (http://www.barbadosparliament.com/the_parliament.php). . Retrieved 2011-11-06.
[11] Garner 2001, p. 177
[12] Salmond 1907, p. 32
[13] Garner 2001, p. 178
[14] "5. The judges are forbidden to pronounce, by way of general and legislative determination, on the causes submitted to them." Code of Napoleon, Decree of March 5, 1803, Law 5 (http://www.napoleon-series.org/research/government/code/book1/c_preliminary.html)
[15] Federal Rule of Civil Procedure, Rule 2 (http://www.law.cornell.edu/rules/frcp/Rule2.htm) ("There is one form of action—the civil action.") (1938)
[16] Friedman 2005, p. xix
[17] "In Suits at common law ... the right of trial by jury shall be preserved, and no fact tried by a jury shall be otherwise reexamined in any Court of the United States, than according to the rules of the common law."
[18] Jefferson, Thomas (February 10, 1814). "Letter to Dr. Thomas Cooper" (http://www.stephenjaygould.org/ctrl/jefferson_cooper.html). . Retrieved 11 July 2012. "Authorities for what is common law may therefore be as well cited, as for any part of the Lex Scripta, and there is no better instance of the necessity of holding the judges and writers to a declaration of their authorities than the present; where we detect them endeavoring to make law where they found none, and to submit us at one stroke to a whole system, no particle of which has its foundation in

the common law. For we know that the common law is that system of law which was introduced by the Saxons on their settlement in England, and altered from time to time by proper legislative authority from that time to the date of Magna Carta, which terminates the period of the common law, or lex non scripta, and commences that of the statute law, or Lex Scripta. This settlement took place about the middle of the fifth century. But Christianity was not introduced till the seventh century; the conversion of the first christian king of the Heptarchy having taken place about the year 598, and that of the last about 686. Here, then, was a space of two hundred years, during which the common law was in existence, and Christianity no part of it."

[19] Jefferson, Thomas (June 5, 1824). "Letter To Major John Cartwright" (http://www.yamaguchy.com/library/jefferson/cartwright.html). . Retrieved 11 July 2012. "I was glad to find in your book a formal contradiction, at length, of the judiciary usurpation of legislative powers; for such the judges have usurped in their repeated decisions, that Christianity is a part of the common law. The proof of the contrary, which you have adduced, is incontrovertible; to wit, that the common law existed while the Anglo-Saxons were yet Pagans, at a time when they had never yet heard the name of Christ pronounced, or knew that such a character had ever existed."

[20] E.g., Lectric Law Dictionary (http://www.lectlaw.com/def/c070.htm) : That which derives its force and authority from the universal consent and immemorial practice of the people.

[21] Some common law is a recent as yesterday's court decisions, and not every practice from "universal consent and immemorial practice" has found its way into "common law."

[22] *e.g.*, *Ex parte Holt*, 19 USPQ2d 1211, 1214 (Bd. Patent App. & Interf. 1991) (explaining the hierarchy of precedent binding on tribunals of the United States Patent Office)

[23] Frederic R. Kellog, Law, Morals, and Justice Holmes, 69 Judicature 214 (1986).

[24] Benjamin N. Cardozo, The Nature of the Judicial Process 22-23 (1921).

[25] The beneficial qualities of the common law's incrementalist evolution was most eloquently expressed by the future Lord Mansfield, then Solicitor General Murray, in the case of *Omychund v. Barker*, who contended that "a statute very seldom can take in all cases; therefore the common law, that works itself pure by rules drawn from the fountain of justice, is for that reason superior to an act of parliament." I Atk. 21, 33, 26 Eng. Rep. 15, 22-23 (Ch. 1744)

[26] *Winterbottom v. Wright*, 10 M&W 109, 152 Eng.Rep. 402, 1842 WL 5519 (Exchequer of pleas 1842)

[27] *Thomas v. Winchester* (http://www.courts.state.ny.us/reporter/archives/thomas_winchester.htm), 6 N.Y. 397 (N.Y. 1852)

[28] *Statler v. Ray Mfg. Co.*, 195 N.Y. 478, 480 (N.Y. 1909)

[29] *Cadillac Motor Car Co. v. Johnson*, 221 F. 801 (2nd Cir. 1915)

[30] *MacPherson v. Buick Motor Co.* (http://www.courts.state.ny.us/reporter/archives/macpherson_buick.htm), 217 N.Y. 382, 111 N.E. 1050 (N.Y. 1916)

[31] *Meister v. Moore*, 96 U.S. 76 (1877) ("No doubt a statute may take away a common law right, but there is always a presumption that the legislature has no such intention unless it be plainly expressed.")

[32] *E.g.*, Uniform Commercial Code, Article 2, on Contracts for the Sales of Goods (http://www.law.cornell.edu/ucc/2/)

[33] Model Penal Code as adopted in several states, for example, New York's Penal Law (http://caselaw.lp.findlaw.com/nycodes/c82.html)

[34] Graham Hughes, Common Law Systems, § VII, Morrison 1996, pp. 23–24

[35] To consider one example, *Lemon v. Kurtzman*, 403 U.S. 602 (1971), resolves one part of the tension between the "establishment" and "free exercise" clauses of the First Amendment with a three part test: a government-sponsored message violates the Establishment Clause if: (1) it does not have a secular purpose; (2) its principal or primary effect advances or inhibits religion; or (3) it creates an excessive entanglement of the government with religion..

[36] https://supreme.justia.com/us/11/32/case.html

[37] *Johnson v. Commonwealth*, 209 Va. 291, 293, 163 S.E.2d 570, ___ (1968)

[38] https://supreme.justia.com/us/5/137/case.html

[39] *E.g.*, *South Corp. v. United States*, 690 F.2d 1368 (Fed. Cir. 1982) (*en banc* in relevant part) (explaining order of precedent binding on the United States Court of Appeals for the Federal Circuit); *Bonner v. City of Prichard, Alabama*, 661 F.2d 1206 (11th Cir. 1981) (*en banc*) (after the Eleventh Circuit was split off from the Fifth Circuit, adopting precedent of Fifth Circuit as binding until overruled by the Eleventh Circuit *en banc*: "The [pre-split] Fifth followed the absolute rule that a prior decision of the circuit (panel or *en banc*) could not be overruled by a panel but only by the court sitting *en banc*. The Eleventh Circuit decides in this case that it chooses, and will follow, this rule."); *Ex parte Holt*, 19 USPQ2d 1211, 1214 (Bd. Patent App. & Interf. 1991) (explaining the hierarchy of precedent binding on tribunals of the United States Patent Office).

[40] 83 Cr App R 191, 73 Cr App R 266

[41] See, e.g., Yeo Tiong Min, " A Note on Some Differences in English Law, New York Law, and Singapore Law (http://www.singaporelaw.sg/content/SomeDifferences.html)" (2006).

[42] Theodore Eisenberg & Geoffrey P. Miller, The Flight to New York: An Empirical Study of Choice of Law and Choice of Forum Clauses in Publicly-Held Companies' Contracts (2008). New York University Law and Economics Working Papers. Paper 124, http://lsr.nellco.org/nyu_lewp/124 (based on a survey of 2882 contracts, "New York law plays a role for major corporate contracts similar to the role Delaware law plays in the limited setting of corporate governance disputes. ... New York's dominance is striking. It is the choice of law in approximately 46 percent of contracts," and if merger contracts excluded, over half)

[43] Eisenberg & Miller at 19-20 (Delaware is chosen in about 15% of contracts, "Delaware dominates for one type of contract – [merger] trust agreements. ... The dominance of Delaware for this specialized type of contract is apparently due to the advantages and flexibility which Delaware's business trust statute.")

[44] Eisenberg & Miller at 19, only about 5% of commercial contracts designate California choice of law, where nearly 50% designate New York.
[45] Osley, Richard (2008-11-23). "London becomes litigation capital of the world" (http://www.independent.co.uk/news/uk/home-news/london-becomes-litigation-capital-of-the-world-1031231.html). *The Independent* (London). .. London is also forum for many defamation cases, because U.K. law is more plaintiff-friendly—in the United States, the First Amendment protection for freedom of the press allows for statements concerning public figures of questionable veracity, where in the U.k., those same statements support a judgment for libel.
[46] U.S. Internal Revenue Service, Taxpayer Advocate Service, 2008 Report to Congress, http://www.irs.gov/pub/irs-utl/08_tas_arc_msp_1.pdf
[47] Outside the law (http://www.nationalarchives.gov.uk/pathways/citizenship/citizen_subject/law.htm) The National Archives
[48] Jeffery, Clarence Ray (1957). "The Development of Crime in Early English Society". *Journal of Criminal Law, Criminology, and Police Science* (The Journal of Criminal Law, Criminology, and Police Science, Vol. 47, No. 6) **47** (6): 647–666. doi:10.2307/1140057. JSTOR 1140057.
[49] Winston Chruchill, *A History of the English Speaking Peoples*, Chapter 13, *The English Common Law*
[50] *see* Oliver Wendell Holmes, Jr., *The Common Law*, Lecture I, sec. 2, "In Massachusetts today...there are some (rules) which can only be understood by reference to the infancy of procedure among the German tribes."
[51] "Common Law". *Catholic Encyclopedia*. New York: Robert Appleton Company. 1913.
[52] William Burnham, *Introduction to the Law and Legal System of the United States*, 4th ed. (St. Paul, Thomson West, 2006), 42.
[53] E.g., *MacPherson v. Buick Motor Co.*, 217 N.Y. 382, 111 N.E. 1050 (N.Y. 1916) (discussed above, adjudicating the tort of negligence that existed in no statute, and expanding the law to cover parties that had never been addressed by statute); Hadley v Baxendale (1854) 9 Exch 341 (defining a new rule of contract law with no basis in statute); *Marbury v. Madison*, 137 5 U.S. 137 (1803) ("It is emphatically the province and duty of the judicial department to say what the law is."); Alexander Hamilton, THE FEDERALIST, Nos. 78 and 81 (J. Cooke ed. 1961), 521–530, 541–55 ("The interpretation of the laws is the proper and peculiar province of the courts. A constitution, is, in fact, and must be regarded by the judges, as a fundamental law. It therefore belongs to them to ascertain its meaning, as well as the meaning of any particular act proceeding from the legislative body."); see rule against perpetuities for a judicially created law originating in 1682 that governs the validity of trusts and future interests in real property, Rule in Shelley's Case for a rule created by judges in 1366 or before, and life estate and fee simple for rules of real property ownership that were judicially created in the late 1100s as the crown began to give law-making power to courts.
[54] *Southern Pacific Co. v. Jensen*, 244 U.S. 205, 221 (1917) (Holmes, J., dissenting).
[55] E.g., R. C. van Caenegem, *The Birth of the English Common Law* 89–92 (1988).
[56] E.g., Peter Birks, Grant McLeod, *Justinian's Institutes* 7 (1987).
[57] E.g., George E. Woodbine (ed.), Samuel E. Thorne (transl.), *Bracton on the Laws and Customs of England*, Vol. I (Introduction) 46 (1968); Carl Güterbock, *Bracton and his Relation to the Roman Law* 35–38 (1866).
[58] Stephen P. Buhofer, *Structuring the Law: The Common Law and the Roman Institutional System*, Swiss Review of International and European Law (SZIER/RSDIE) 5/2007, 24 (download at http://www.szier.ch - archive).
[59] Peter Stein, *Continental Influences on English Legal thought, 1600–1900, in* Peter Stein, *The Character and Influence of the Roman Civil Law* 223 *et seq.* (1988).
[60] See generally Stephen P. Buhofer, *Structuring the Law: The Common Law and the Roman Institutional System*, Swiss Review of International and European Law (SZIER/RSDIE) 5/2007 (download at http://www.szier.ch - archive).
[61] Lammi, Glenn G.; Chang, James (December 17, 2004). "Michigan High Court Ruling Offers Positive Guidance on Challenges to Tort Reform Laws" (http://www.wlf.org/upload/121704LBChang.pdf). *Legal Backgrounder* (Washington Legal Foundation) **19** (46). ISBN 10563059. .
[62] *Milestones! 200 Years of American Law: Milestones in Our Legal History*. By Jethro Koller Lieberman. Published by West, 1976. Original from the University of California. Digitized Jun 11, 2008. ISBN 0-19-519881-6, ISBN 978-0-19-519881-2, pg. 16 (http://books.google.com/books?id=i_2wAAAAIAAJ&pgis=1)
[63] New York Constitution of 1777 (http://www.yale.edu/lawweb/avalon/states/ny01.htm) via Avalon Project at Yale Law School.
[64] Alexander Hamilton, Federalist 84 (http://www.constitution.org/fed/federa84.htm) (1788).
[65] Nathan Dane, 6 *General Abridgment and Digest of American Law* §182, art. 5, 230 (Cummings, Hilliard & Co. 1823).
[66] *Washington Legal Foundation v. Legal Foundation of Washington*, 271 F.3d 835 (http://laws.lp.findlaw.com/getcase/9th/case/9835154&exact=1) (9th Cir. 2001).
[67] Quebec North Shore Paper Co. v. Canadian Pacific (1976), [1977] 2 S.C.R 1054; St-Hilaire v. Canada (Attorney General), 2001 FCA 63, [2001] 4 FC 289
[68] *An Act to repeal certain parts of an Act passed in the Fourteenth Year of His Majesty's Reign, intituled an Act for making more effectual Provision for the Government of the Province of Quebec in North America; and to introduce the English Law, as the Rule of Decision in all matters of controversy relative to Property and Civil Rights*, S.U.C. 1792 (32 Geo. III), c. 1.
[69] *The North-West Territories Act* (http://www.qp.gov.sk.ca/documents/english/statutes/historical/NWT.pdf), R.S.C.1885, c. 50, s. 11.
[70] *Alberta Act* (http://www.solon.org/Constitutions/Canada/English/aa_1905.html), S.C. 1905, c. 3, s. 16.
[71] *Saskatchewan Act* (http://www.qp.gov.sk.ca/documents/english/statutes/historical/SK Act.pdf), S.C. 1905, c. 42, s. 16.
[72] "Chapter I, Section 8 of Hong Kong Basic Law" (http://www.basiclaw.gov.hk/en/basiclawtext/chapter_1.html). Basiclaw.gov.hk. 2008-03-17. . Retrieved 2010-05-30.

[73] Holmes, Jr., Oliver Wendell (1897). "The Path of the Law" (http://www.gutenberg.org/ebooks/2373). *Harvard Law Review* **10** (8): 457, 469. doi:10.2307/1322028. .
[74] *Acree v. Republic of Iraq*, 370 F.3d 41 (D.C. Cir. 2004) (Roberts, J., concurring).
[75] Salmond 1907, p. 34
[76] Lobban, M. (2004). "Preparing for Fusion: Reforming the Nineteenth-Century Court of Chancery, Part II" (http://www.historycooperative.org/journals/lhr/22.3/forum_lobban.html#FOOT142). *Law and History Review*. University of Illinois. .
[77] *E.g.*, *Markman v. Westview Instruments, Inc.*, 517 U.S. 370, 376 (1996) ("[W]e [the U.S. Supreme Court] have understood that the right of trial by jury thus preserved is the right which existed under the English common law when the Amendment was adopted. In keeping with our longstanding adherence to this 'historical test,' we ask, first, whether we are dealing with a cause of action that either was tried at law at the time of the founding or is at least analogous to one that was. If the action in question belongs in the law category, we then ask whether the particular trial decision must fall to the jury in order to preserve the substance of the common-law right as it existed in 1791." citations and quotations omitted, holding that interpretation of the scope of a patent had no analogy in 1790, and is thus a question to be decided by a judge, not a jury)
[78] John Jay McKelvey, Principles of Common Law Pleading (1894).
[79] Note that the remainder of the "common law" discussed in the rest of the article remained intact; all that was abolished were the highly technical requirements for language of the paper provided by the plaintiff to the defendant to initiate a case.
[80] At least in the U.S., practicing lawyers tend to use "law professor" or "law review article" as a pejorative to describe a person or work that is insufficiently grounded in reality or practicality – every young lawyer is admonished repeatedly by senior lawyers not to write "law review articles," but instead to focus on the facts of the case and the practical effects of a given outcome.
[81] http://caselaw.lp.findlaw.com/scripts/getcase.pl?navby=CASE&court=US&vol=304&page=64
[82] *Swift v. Tyson*, 41 U.S. 1 (http://caselaw.lp.findlaw.com/scripts/getcase.pl?navby=CASE&court=US&vol=41&page=1) (1842). In *Swift*, the United States Supreme Court had held that federal courts hearing cases brought under their diversity jurisdiction (allowing them to hear cases between parties from different states) had to apply the statutory law of the states, but not the common law developed by state courts. Instead, the Supreme Court permitted the federal courts to make their own common law based on general principles of law. *Erie v. Tompkins*, 304 U.S. 64 (http://caselaw.lp.findlaw.com/scripts/getcase.pl?navby=CASE&court=US&vol=304&page=64) (1938). *Erie* overruled *Swift v. Tyson*, and instead held that federal courts exercising diversity jurisdiction had to use all of the same substantive law as the courts of the states in which they were located. As the *Erie* Court put it, there is no "general federal common law", the key word here being ***general***. This history is elaborated in federal common law.
[83] https://supreme.justia.com/us/451/630/case.html
[84] https://supreme.justia.com/us/318/363/case.html
[85] http://caselaw.lp.findlaw.com/scripts/getcase.pl?navby=CASE&court=US&vol=248&page=215
[86] *City of Boerne v. Flores*, 521 U.S. 507 (http://caselaw.lp.findlaw.com/scripts/getcase.pl?court=us&vol=521&invol=507) (1997) (invalidating the Religious Freedom Restoration Act, in which Congress had attempted to redefine the court's jurisdiction to decide constitutional issues); *Milwaukee v. Illinois*, 451 U.S. 304 (http://caselaw.lp.findlaw.com/scripts/getcase.pl?court=us&vol=451&invol=304) (1981)
[87] Glenn 2000, p. 255
[88] Glenn 2000, p. 276
[89] Alexander, C.H. (July 1952). "International Law in India". *The International and Comparative Law Quarterly* **1** (3): 289–300. ISSN 0020-5893.
[90] Viswanatha, S.T., *International Law in Ancient India*, 1925
[91] Glenn 2000, p. 273
[92] Jain 2006, p. 2
[93] "Indian Legislation" (http://www.commonlii.org/in/legis/num_act/). Commonlii.org. . Retrieved 2010-05-30.
[94] http://www.fca-caf.gc.ca/index_e.shtml
[95] The division of jurisdiction between the federal and provincial Parliaments is specified in the Canadian constitution. Constitution Act, 1867 (http://laws.justice.gc.ca/eng/Const/page-5.html#anchorbo-ga:s_91-gb:s_91), s. 91(10), (18)
[96] "Canadian Legislative Bijuralism Site At the Crossroads of our Legal Diversity" (http://canada.justice.gc.ca/eng/bijurilex/index.html). Canada.justice.gc.ca. 2009-08-05. . Retrieved 2010-05-30.
[97] Mahler, Gregory S. (2004). *Politics and Government in Israel: The Maturation of a Modern State*. New York: Rowman & Littlefield. p. 126. ISBN 0-7425-611-3.
[98] http://eur-lex.europa.eu/LexUriServ/LexUriServ.do?uri=CELEX:61981J0283:EN:NOT

Further reading

- Friedman, Lawrence Meir (2005). *A History of American Law* (http://books.google.com/books?id=JndnEiydTiYC&pg=PR19) (3rd ed.). New York: Simon and Schuster. ISBN 978-0-7432-8258-1.
- Garner, Bryan A. (2001). *A Dictionary of Modern Legal Usage* (http://books.google.com/books?id=35dZpfMmxqsC&pg=PA178) (2nd, revised ed.). New York: Oxford University Press. ISBN 978-0-19-514236-5.
- Morrison, Alan B. (1996). *Fundamentals of American Law* (http://books.google.com/books?id=Si0lupMPrEoC&pg=PA23). New York: Oxford University Press. ISBN 978-0-19-876405-2.
- Salmond, John William (1907). *Jurisprudence: The Theory of the Law* (http://books.google.com/books?id=i2gaAAAAYAAJ&pg=PA32) (2nd ed.). London: Stevens and Haynes. OCLC 1384458.

External links

- *The Common Law* (http://biotech.law.lsu.edu/Books/Holmes/claw_c.htm) by Oliver Wendell Holmes, Jr.
- *The Common Law by Oliver Wendell Holmes Jr.* at Project Gutenberg
- The History of the Common Law of England by Matthew Hale (http://www.bdlawservice.com/books/the_history.pdf)
- The Australian Institute of Comparative Legal Systems (http://ausicl.com)
- The International Institute for Law and Strategic Studies (IILSS) (http://www.iilss.org)
- *New South Wales Legislation* (http://legislation.nsw.gov.au)
- Historical Laws of Hong Kong Online (http://xml.lib.hku.hk/gsdl/db/oelawhk/search.shtml) – University of Hong Kong Libraries, Digital Initiatives
- Maxims of Common Law (http://www.lawfulpath.com/ref/bouvier/maxims.shtml) from Bouvier's 1856 Law Dictionary

Cinchocaine

Cinchocaine

[[file:Cinchocaine.svg	alt=]]
Systematic (IUPAC) name	
2-butoxy-*N*-[2-(diethylamino)ethyl]quinoline-4-carboxamide	
Clinical data	
AHFS/Drugs.com	International Drug Names [1]
Pregnancy cat.	?
Legal status	?
Routes	topical, intravenous (equine euthanasia)
Identifiers	
CAS number	85-79-0 [2] ✓
ATC code	C05AD04 [3] D04AB02 [4] N01BB06 [5] S01HA06 [6] S02DA04 [7]
PubChem	CID 3025 [8]
DrugBank	DB00527 [9]
ChemSpider	2917 [10] ✓
UNII	L6JW2TJG99 [11] ✓
KEGG	D00733 [12] ✓
ChEBI	CHEBI:247956 [13] ✓
ChEMBL	CHEMBL1086 [14] ✓
Chemical data	
Formula	$C_{20}H_{29}N_3O_2$
Mol. mass	343.463 g/mol
✓ **(what is this?) (verify)** [15]	

Dibucaine or **cinchocaine** is an amide local anesthetic. Among the most potent and toxic of the long-acting local anesthetics, current use of dibucaine is generally restricted to spinal and topical anesthesia.[16] [17]

Physical properties

Dibucaine is relatively insoluble in alkaline aquatic solutions.

Brand names

It is sold under the brand names **Cincain**, **Nupercainal**, **Nupercaine** and **Sovcaine**. It is the active ingredient in some topical hemorrhoid creams such as Proctosedyl. It is also a component of the veterinary drug **Somulose**, used for euthanasia of horses and cattle.

See also

- Dibucaine number

References

[1] http://www.drugs.com/international/cinchocaine.html
[2] http://www.nlm.nih.gov/cgi/mesh/2009/MB_cgi?term=85-79-0&rn=1
[3] http://www.whocc.no/atc_ddd_index/?code=C05AD04
[4] http://www.whocc.no/atc_ddd_index/?code=D04AB02
[5] http://www.whocc.no/atc_ddd_index/?code=N01BB06
[6] http://www.whocc.no/atc_ddd_index/?code=S01HA06
[7] http://www.whocc.no/atc_ddd_index/?code=S02DA04
[8] http://pubchem.ncbi.nlm.nih.gov/summary/summary.cgi?cid=3025
[9] http://www.drugbank.ca/drugs/DB00527
[10] http://www.chemspider.com/Chemical-Structure.2917
[11] http://fdasis.nlm.nih.gov/srs/srsdirect.jsp?regno=L6JW2TJG99
[12] http://www.kegg.jp/entry/D00733
[13] https://www.ebi.ac.uk/chebi/searchId.do?chebiId=CHEBI:247956
[14] https://www.ebi.ac.uk/chembldb/index.php/compound/inspect/CHEMBL1086
[15] http://en.wikipedia.org/wiki/Special%3Acomparepages
[16] Martindale, The Extra Pharmacopoeia, 30th ed, p1006
[17] Dibucaine (http://www.nlm.nih.gov/cgi/mesh/2009/MB_cgi?mode=&term=Dibucaine)

Further reading

- Abdel-Ghani N, Youssef A, Awady M (2005). "Cinchocaine hydrochloride determination by atomic absorption spectrometry and spectrophotometry.". *Farmaco* **60** (5): 419–24. doi:10.1016/j.farmac.2005.03.001. PMID 15910814.
- Souto-Padron T, Lima AP, de Oliveira Ribeiro R. (2006). "Effects of dibucaine on the endocytic/exocytic pathways in Trypanosoma cruzi.". *Parasitol Res* **99** (4): 317. doi:10.1007/s00436-006-0192-1. PMID 16612626.
- Nounou M, El-Khordagui L, Khalafallah N (2005). "Effect of various formulation variables on the encapsulation and stability of dibucaine base in multilamellar vesicles.". *Acta Pol Pharm* **62** (5): 369–79. PMID 16459486.
- Aroti,A.;Leontidis, E. (2001). *Journal of Chemical Education* **76**: 786–788.

Lumbar puncture

Lumbar puncture	
Intervention	
A patient undergoes a lumbar puncture at the hands of a neurologist. The reddish-brown swirls on the patient's back are tincture of iodine (an antiseptic).	
ICD-9-CM	03.31 [1]
MeSH	D013129 [2]

A **lumbar puncture** (or **LP**, and colloquially known as a **spinal tap**) is a diagnostic and at times therapeutic procedure that is performed in order to collect a sample of cerebrospinal fluid (CSF) for biochemical, microbiological, and cytological analysis, or very rarely as a treatment ("therapeutic lumbar puncture") to relieve increased intracranial pressure.

Indications

The most common purpose for a lumbar puncture is to collect cerebrospinal fluid in a case of suspected meningitis, since there is no other reliable tool with which meningitis, a life-threatening but highly treatable condition, can be excluded. Young infants commonly require lumbar puncture as a part of the routine workup for fever without a source, as they have a much higher risk of meningitis than older persons and do not reliably show signs of meningeal irritation (meningismus). In any age group, subarachnoid hemorrhage, hydrocephalus, benign intracranial hypertension and many other diagnoses may be supported or excluded with this test.

Lumbar punctures may also be done to inject medications into the cerebrospinal fluid ("intrathecally"), particularly for spinal anesthesia or chemotherapy. It may also be used to detect the presence of malignant cells in the CSF, as in carcinomatous meningitis or medulloblastoma.

Contraindications

Lumbar puncture should not be performed in the following situations

- Idiopathic (unidentified cause) increased intracranial pressure (ICP)
  - Rationale: lumbar puncture in the presence of increased ICP may cause uncal herniation
  - Exception: therapeutic use of lumbar puncture to reduce ICP
  - Precaution
    - CT brain is advocated by some, especially in the following situations
      - Age >65
      - Reduced GCS or conscious state
      - Recent history of seizure
      - Focal neurological signs
    - Ophthalmoscopy for papilledema
- Bleeding diathesis
  - Coagulopathy
  - Decreased platelet count (<50 x 10^9/L)
- Infections[3]
  - Skin infection at puncture site
  - Sepsis

- Abnormal respiratory pattern
- Hypertension with bradycardia and deteriorating consciousness
- Vertebral deformities (scoliosis or kyphosis), in hands of an inexperienced physician.[4] [5]

Procedure

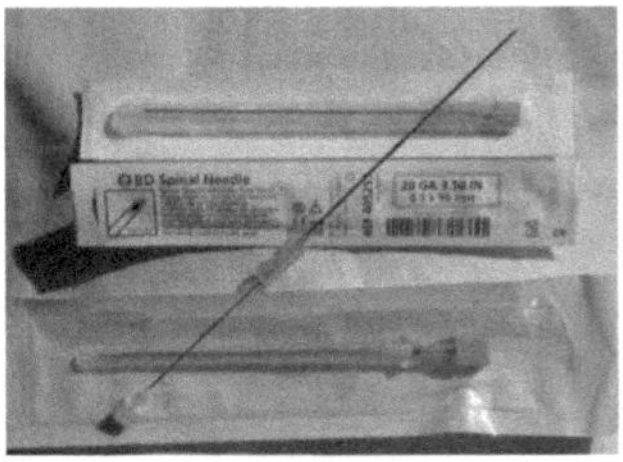
Spinal needles used in lumbar puncture.

In performing a lumbar puncture, first the patient is usually placed in a left (or right) lateral position with his/her neck bent in full flexion and knees bent in full flexion up to his/her chest, approximating a fetal position as much as possible. It is also possible to have the patient sit on a stool and bend his/her head and shoulders forward. The area around the lower back is prepared using aseptic technique. Once the appropriate location is palpated, local anaesthetic is infiltrated under the skin and then injected along the intended path of the spinal needle. A spinal needle is inserted between the lumbar vertebrae L3/L4 or L4/L5 and pushed in until there is a "give" that indicates the needle is past the ligamentum flavum. The needle is again pushed until there is a second 'give' that indicates the needle is now past the dura mater. Since the arachnoid membrane and the dura mater exist in flush contact with one another in the living person's spine (due to fluid pressure from CSF in the subarachnoid space pushing the arachnoid membrane out towards the dura), once the needle has pierced the dura mater it has also traversed the thinner arachnoid membrane and is now in the subarachnoid space. The stylet from the spinal needle is then withdrawn and drops of cerebrospinal fluid are collected. The opening pressure of the cerebrospinal fluid may be taken during this collection by using a simple column manometer. The procedure is ended by withdrawing the needle while placing pressure on the puncture site. In the past, the patient would often be asked to lie on his/her back for at least six hours and be monitored for signs of neurological problems, though there is no scientific evidence that this provides any benefit. The technique described is almost identical to that used in spinal anesthesia, except that spinal anesthesia is more often done with the patient in a seated position.

The upright seated position is advantageous in that there is less distortion of spinal anatomy which allows for easier withdrawal of fluid. It is preferred by some practitioners when a lumbar puncture is performed on an obese patient where having them lie on their side would cause a scoliosis and unreliable anatomical landmarks. On the other hand, opening pressures are notoriously unreliable when measured on a seated patient and therefore the left or right lateral (lying down) position is preferred if an opening pressure needs to be measured.

Patient anxiety during the procedure can lead to increased CSF pressure, especially if the person holds their breath, tenses their muscles or flexes their knees too tightly against their chest. Diagnostic analysis of changes in fluid pressure during lumbar puncture procedures requires attention both to the patient's condition during the procedure and to their medical history.

Reinsertion of the stylet may decrease the rate of post lumbar puncture headaches.[5]

Risks

Post spinal headache with nausea is the most common complication; it often responds to analgesics and infusion of fluids. It was long taught that this complication can often be prevented by strict maintenance of a supine posture for two hours after the successful puncture; this has not been borne out in modern studies involving large numbers of patients. *Merritt's Neurology* (10th edition), in the section on lumbar puncture, notes that intravenous caffeine injection is often quite effective in aborting these so-called "spinal headaches." Contact between the side of the lumbar puncture needle and a spinal nerve root can result in anomalous sensations (paresthesia) in a leg during the procedure; this is harmless and patients can be warned about it in advance to minimize their anxiety if it should occur. A headache that is persistent despite a long period of bedrest and occurs only when sitting up may be indicative of a CSF leak from the lumbar puncture site. It can be treated by more bedrest, or by an epidural blood patch, where the patient's own blood is injected back into the site of leakage to cause a clot to form and seal off the leak.

Serious complications of a properly performed lumbar puncture are extremely rare. They include spinal or epidural bleeding, adhesive arachnoiditis and trauma to the spinal cord or spinal nerve roots resulting in weakness or loss of sensation, or even paraplegia. The latter is exceedingly rare, since the level at which the spinal cord ends (normally the inferior border of L1, although it is slightly lower in infants) is several vertebral spaces above the proper location for a lumbar puncture (L3/L4). There are case reports of lumbar puncture resulting in perforation of abnormal dural arterio-venous malformations, resulting in catastrophic epidural hemorrhage; this is exceedingly rare.

The procedure is not recommended when epidural infection is present or suspected, when topical infections or dermatological conditions pose a risk of infection at the puncture site or in patients with severe psychosis or neurosis with back pain. Some authorities believe that withdrawal of fluid when initial pressures are abnormal could result in spinal cord compression or cerebral herniation; others believe that such events are merely coincidental in time, occurring independently as a result of the same pathology that the lumbar puncture was performed to diagnose. In any case, computed tomography of the brain is often performed prior to lumbar puncture if an intracranial mass is suspected.

Removal of cerebrospinal fluid resulting in reduced fluid pressure has been shown to correlate with greater reduction of cerebral blood flow among patients with Alzheimer's disease. Its clinical significance is uncertain.

Diagnostics

Increased CSF pressure can indicate congestive heart failure, cerebral edema, subarachnoid hemorrhage, hypo-osmolality resulting from hemodialysis, meningeal inflammation, purulent meningitis or tuberculous meningitis, hydrocephalus, or pseudotumor cerebri.

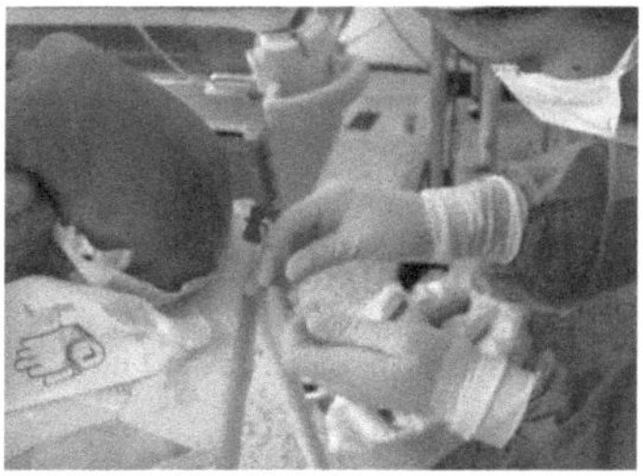
Lumbar puncture in a child suspected of having meningitis.

Decreased CSF pressure can indicate complete subarachnoid blockage, leakage of spinal fluid, severe dehydration, hyperosmolality, or circulatory collapse. Significant changes in pressure during the procedure can indicate tumors or spinal blockage resulting in a large pool of CSF, or hydrocephalus associated with large volumes of CSF. Lumbar puncture for the purpose of reducing pressure is performed in some patients with idiopathic intracranial hypertension (also called pseudotumor cerebri.)

The presence of white blood cells in cerebrospinal fluid is called pleocytosis. A small number of monocytes can be normal; the presence of granulocytes is always an abnormal finding. A large number of granulocytes often heralds bacterial meningitis. White cells can also indicate reaction to repeated lumbar punctures, reactions to prior injections of medicines or dyes, central nervous system hemorrhage, leukemia, recent epileptic seizure, or a metastatic tumor. When peripheral blood contaminates the withdrawn CSF, a common procedural complication, white blood cells will be present along with erythrocytes, and their ratio will be the same as that in the peripheral blood.

The finding of erythrophagocytosis,[6] where phagocytosed erythrocytes is observed, signifies haemorrhage into the CSF that preceded the lumbar puncture. Therefore, when erythrocytes are detected in the CSF sample, erythrophagocytosis suggests causes other than a traumatic tap, such as intracranial haemorrhage and haemorrhagic herpetic encephalitis. In which case, further investigations are warranted, including imaging and viral culture.

Several substances found in cerebrospinal fluid are available for diagnostic measurement.

- Measurement of chloride levels may aid in detecting the presence of tuberculous meningitis.
- Glucose is usually present in the CSF; the level is usually about 60% that in the peripheral circulation. A fingerstick or venipuncture at the time of lumbar puncture may therefore be performed to assess peripheral glucose levels in order to determine a predicted CSF glucose value. Decreased glucose levels can indicate fungal, tuberculous or pyogenic infections; lymphomas; leukemia spreading to the meninges; meningoencephalitic mumps; or hypoglycemia. A glucose level of less than one third of blood glucose levels in association with low CSF lactate levels is typical in hereditary CSF glucose transporter deficiency also known as De Vivo disease.
- Increased glucose levels in the fluid can indicate diabetes, although the 60% rule still applies.
- Increased levels of glutamine are often involved with hepatic encephalopathies, Reye's syndrome, hepatic coma, cirrhosis and hypercapnia.
- Increased levels of lactate can occur the presence of cancer of the CNS, multiple sclerosis, heritable mitochondrial disease, low blood pressure, low serum phosphorus, respiratory alkalosis, idiopathic seizures, traumatic brain injury, cerebral ischemia, brain abscess, hydrocephalus, hypocapnia or bacterial meningitis.
- The enzyme lactate dehydrogenase can be measured to help distinguish meningitides of bacterial origin, which are often associated with high levels of the enzyme, from those of viral origin in which the enzyme is low or absent.
- Changes in total protein content of cerebrospinal fluid can result from pathologically increased permeability of the blood-cerebrospinal fluid barrier, obstructions of CSF circulation, meningitis, neurosyphilis, brain abscesses, subarachnoid hemorrhage, polio, collagen disease or Guillain-Barré syndrome, leakage of CSF, increases in intracranial pressure or hyperthyroidism. Very high levels of protein may indicate tuberculous meningitis or spinal block.
- IgG synthetic rate is calculated from measured IgG and total protein levels; it is elevated in immune disorders such as multiple sclerosis, transverse myelitis, and neuromyelitis optica of Devic.
- Numerous antibody-mediated tests for CSF are available in some countries: these include rapid tests for antigens of common bacterial pathogens, treponemal titers for the diagnosis of neurosyphilis and Lyme disease, Coccidioides antibody, and others.
- The India ink test is still used for detection of meningitis caused by Cryptococcus neoformans, but the cryptococcal antigen (CrAg) test has a higher sensitivity.
- CSF can be sent to the microbiology lab for various types of smears and cultures to diagnose infections.
- Polymerase chain reaction (PCR) has been a great advance in the diagnosis of some types of meningitis. It has high sensitivity and specificity for many infections of the CNS, is fast, and can be done with small volumes of CSF. Even though testing is expensive, it saves cost of hospitalization.

History

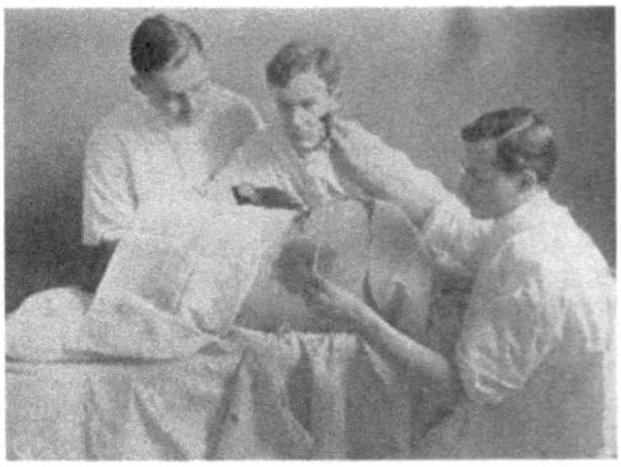

Lumbar puncture, early 20th century.

The first technique for accessing the dural space was described by the London physician Walter Essex Wynter. In 1889 he developed a crude cut down with cannulation in four patients with tuberculous meningitis. The main purpose was the treatment of raised intracranial pressure rather than for diagnosis.[7] The technique for needle lumbar puncture was then introduced by the German physician Heinrich Quincke, who credits Wynter with the earlier discovery; he first reported his experiences at an internal medicine conference in Wiesbaden, Germany, in 1891.[8] He subsequently published a book on the subject.[9] [10]

The lumbar puncture procedure was taken to the United States by Arthur H. Wentworth an assistant professor at the Harvard Medical School, based at Children's Hospital. In 1893 he published a long paper on diagnosing cerebrospinal meningitis by examining spinal fluid. His career took a nosedive, however, when antivivisectionists prosecuted him for having obtained spinal fluid from children. He was acquitted, but he was uninvited from the then forming Johns Hopkins School of Medicine, where he would have been the first professor of pediatrics.

References

[1] http://icd9cm.chrisendres.com/index.php?srchtype=procs&srchtext=03.31&Submit=Search&action=search

[2] http://www.nlm.nih.gov/cgi/mesh/2011/MB_cgi?field=uid&term=D013129

[3] Mary Louise Turgeon (2005). *Clinical hematology: theory and procedures* (http://books.google.com/books?id=cHAjsUgegpQC&pg=PA401). Lippincott Williams & Wilkins. pp. 401–. ISBN 978-0-7817-5007-3. . Retrieved 28 October 2010.

[4] Roos KL (March 2003). "Lumbar puncture". *Semin Neurol* **23** (1): 105–14. doi:10.1055/s-2003-40758. PMID 12870112.

[5] Straus SE, Thorpe KE, Holroyd-Leduc J (October 2006). "How do I perform a lumbar puncture and analyze the results to diagnose bacterial meningitis?". *JAMA* **296** (16): 2012–22. doi:10.1001/jama.296.16.2012. PMID 17062865.

[6] Harald Kluge (2007). *Atlas of CSF cytology* (http://books.google.com/books?id=HDLv-LAfqHoC&pg=PA45). Thieme. pp. 45–46. ISBN 978-3-13-143161-5. . Retrieved 28 October 2010.

[7] Wynter W. E. (1891). "Four Cases of Tubercular Meningitis in Which Paracentesis of the Theca Vertebralis Was Performed for the Relief of Fluid Pressure". *Lancet* **1** (3531): 981–2. doi:10.1016/S0140-6736(02)16784-5.

[8] Quincke HI (1891). *Verhandlungen des Congresses für Innere Medizin, Zehnter Congress, Wiesbaden*. **10**. pp. 321–331.

[9] Quincke HI (1902). *Die Technik der Lumbalpunktion*. Berlin & Vienna.

[10] *Heinrich Irenaeus Quincke* (http://www.whonamedit.com/doctor.cfm/504.html) at Who Named It?

External links

- eMedicine: Lumbar puncture (http://www.emedicine.com/neuro/topic557.htm)
- Medstudents: Procedures: Lumbar puncture (http://www.medstudents.com.br/proced/lumbpunc.htm)
- Video of lumbar puncture (http://nursinggazette.blogspot.com/2007/10/lumbar-puncture-video.html)

Paraplegia

Paraplegia	
Classification and external resources	
ICD-10	G82.1 [1]
ICD-9	334.1 [2], 344.1 [3]
MeSH	[4]

Paraplegia is an impairment in motor or sensory function of the lower extremities. The word comes from Ionic Greek: παραπληγίη "half-striking". It is usually caused by spinal cord injury or a congenital condition such as spina bifida that affects the neural elements of the spinal canal. The area of the spinal canal that is affected in paraplegia is either the thoracic, lumbar, or sacral regions. If all four limbs are affected by paralysis, quadriplegia is the proper terminology. If only one limb is affected, the correct term is monoplegia.

Spastic paraplegia is a form of paraplegia defined by spasticity of the affected muscles, rather than flaccid paralysis.

Complications

Due to the decrease or loss of feeling or function in the lower extremities, paraplegia can contribute to a number of medical complications including pressure sores (decubitus), thrombosis, and pneumonia. Physiotherapy and various assistive technology, such as a standing frame, as well as vigilant self-observation and -care, may aid in helping to prevent future complications and mitigate existing complications.

As paraplegia is most often the result of a traumatic injury to the spinal cord tissue and the resulting inflammation, other nerve-related complications can and do occur. Cases of chronic nerve pain in the areas surrounding the point of injury are not uncommon. There is speculation that the "phantom pains" experienced by individuals suffering from paralysis could be a direct result of these collateral nerve injuries misinterpreted by the brain.

Treatment

Individuals with paraplegia can range in their level of disability, requiring treatments to vary from case to case. From a rehabilitation standpoint, the most important factor is to gain as much functionality and independence back as possible. Physiotherapists spend many hours within a rehabilitation setting working on strength, range of motion/stretching and transfer skills.[5] Wheelchair mobility is also an important skill to learn. Most paraplegics will be dependent on a wheelchair as a mode of transportation. Thus it is extremely important to teach them the basic skills to gain their independence.[6] Activities of daily living (ADLs) can be quite challenging at first for those with a spinal cord injury (SCI). With the aid of physiotherapists and occupational therapists, individuals with an SCI can learn new skills and adapt previous ones to maximize independence, often living independently within the community.[7]

See also

- Hemiplegia
- Quadriplegia
- Cauda equina syndrome
- *The Body Silent*

References

[1] http://apps.who.int/classifications/icd10/browse/2010/en#/G82.1
[2] http://www.icd9data.com/getICD9Code.ashx?icd9=334.1
[3] http://www.icd9data.com/getICD9Code.ashx?icd9=344.1
[4] http://www.nlm.nih.gov/cgi/mesh//MB_cgi?
[5] Taylor-Schroeder S, LaBarbera J, McDowell S, *et al.* (2011). "The SCIRehab project: treatment time spent in SCI rehabilitation. Physical therapy treatment time during inpatient spinal cord injury rehabilitation" (http://openurl.ingenta.com/content/nlm?genre=article&issn=1079-0268&volume=34&issue=2&spage=149&aulast=Taylor-Schroeder). *J Spinal Cord Med* **34** (2): 149–61. PMC 3066500. PMID 21675354. .
[6] Ozelie R, Sipple C, Foy T, *et al.* (2009). "SCIRehab Project series: the occupational therapy taxonomy". *J Spinal Cord Med* **32** (3): 283–97. PMC 2718817. PMID 19810630.
[7] Tzonichaki I, Kleftaras G (2002). "Paraplegia from spinal cord injury: self-esteem, loneliness, and life satisfaction" (http://psycnet.apa.org/psycinfo/2002-17664-001). *OTJR: Occupation, Participation and Health* **22** (3): 96–103. .

Standard of care

For the English law, see standard of care in English law.

In tort law, the **standard of care** is the degree of prudence and caution required of an individual who is under a duty of care.

The requirements of the standard are closely dependent on circumstances. Whether the standard of care has been breached is determined by the trier of fact, and is usually phrased in terms of the reasonable person. It was famously described in *Vaughn v. Menlove* (1837) as whether the individual "proceed[ed] with such reasonable caution as a prudent man would have exercised under such circumstances."

Professional standard of care

In certain industries and professions, the standard of care is determined by the standard that would be exercised by the reasonably prudent manufacturer of a product, or the reasonably prudent professional in that line of work. Such a test (known as the 'Bolam Test') is used to determine whether a doctor is liable for medical malpractice. The standard of care is important because it determines the level of negligence required to state a valid cause of action.

Medical standard of care

A **standard of care** is a medical or psychological treatment guideline, and can be general or specific. It specifies appropriate treatment based on scientific evidence and collaboration between medical and/or psychological professionals involved in the treatment of a given condition.

Some common examples include:

- Treatment standards applied within public hospitals to ensure that all patients receive appropriate care regardless of financial means.
- Standards of Care for the Health of Transsexual, Transgender, and Gender Nonconforming People

1. Diagnostic and treatment process that a clinician should follow for a certain type of patient, illness, or clinical circumstance. Adjuvant chemotherapy for lung cancer is "a new standard of care, but not necessarily the only

standard of care." (*New England Journal of Medicine*, 2004)

2. In legal terms, the level at which an ordinary, prudent professional having the same training and experience in good standing in a same or similar community would practice under the same or similar circumstances. An "average" standard would not apply because in that case at least half of any group of practitioners would not qualify. The medical malpractice plaintiff must establish the appropriate standard of care and demonstrate that the standard of care has been breached, with expert testimony.

3. A physician also has a "duty to inform" a patient of any material risks or fiduciary interests of the physician that might cause the patient to reconsider a procedure, and may be liable if injury occurs due to the undisclosed risk, and the patient can prove that if he had been informed he would not have gone through with the procedure, without benefit of hindsight. (Informed Consent Rule.) Full disclosure of all material risks incident to treatment must be fully disclosed, unless doing so would impair urgent treatment. As it relates to mental health professionals standard of care, the California Supreme Court, held that these professionals have "duty to protect" individuals who are specifically threatened by a patient. [Tarasoff v. Regents of the University of California, 17 Cal. 3d 425, 551 P.2d 334, 131 Cal. Rptr. 14 (Cal. 1976)].

4. A recipient of *pro bono* (free) services (either legal or medical) is entitled to expect the same standard of care as a person who pays for the same services, to prevent an indigent person from being entitled to only substandard care.

Medical standards of care exist for many conditions, including diabetes, some cancers, and sexual abuse.

Children

A special standard of care also applies to children, who, in a majority of jurisdictions, are held to the behavior that is reasonable for a child of similar age, experience, and intelligence under like circumstances. (Restatement (Second) of Torts §283A; *Cleveland Rolling-Mill Co. v. Corrigan*, 46 Ohio St. 283, 20 N.E. 466 (1889).) In some cases it means that more may be required of a child of superior intelligence. (Compare *Jones v. Fireman's Insurance Co. of Newark, New Jersey*, 240 So.2d 780 [La.App. 1970] with *Robinson v. Travis*, 393 So.2d 304 (La.App. 1980). An exception is for children engaged in "adult activity." *Dellwo v. Pearson*, 107 N.W.2d 859 (Minn 1961) *Nicholsen v. Brown*, 232 Or. 426, 374 P.2d 896 (1962) (automobile); *Daniels v. Evans*, 102 N.H. 407, 224 A. 2d 63 (1966) (motor scooter); *Neumann. v. Shlansky*, 58 Misc. 2d 128, 294 N.Y.S.2d 628 (1968 (playing golf)) What constitutes an "adult standard" may depend on local statute, and some have arbitrary age distinctions. Another exception is if the child is engaged in an "inherently dangerous activity." It is up to the trier of fact to decide if the activity is inherently dangerous. If they find that it is, the child must be held to an adult standard of care. *Robinson v. Lindsay*, 92 Wash.2d 410, 598 P.2d 2392 (1979) (snowmobile);

Persons with disabilities

A person with a disability is held to the same standard of care that an ordinary reasonable person would observe if he suffered from that same disability. (*Roberts v. State of Louisiana*, 396 So.2d 566 (1981) (blind postal employee)) However, courts do not recognize a person with a *mental* disability to be subject to any such special standard, and are held to the "reasonable prudent person" standard, except when the onset of mental illness is unforeseeable and sudden (e.g., *Breunig v. American Family Insurance Co.*, 45 Wis.2d 536, 173 N.W.2d 619 (1970) (sudden hallucinations while driving).) In some situations, this could work an injustice. Physical handicaps and infirmities, such as blindness, deafness, short stature, or a club foot, or the weaknesses of age or sex, are treated merely as part of the “circumstances” under which a reasonable man must act.

Duty to inform self of responsibilities

A person engaged in a special and potentially dangerous activity must know or inquire of possible hazards or of any special duties and responsibilities inherent in that activity that might affect their ability to exercise reasonable prudent caution (*cf, Delair v. McAdoo*, 324 Pa. 392, 188 A. 181 (1936) (driving on worn tires).) Custom and practice of usage may be useful evidence for determining the usual standard, but not determinative of what a reasonable prudent person *ought* to be required to do or know (cf., *Trimarco v. Klein*, 58 N.Y. 2d 98 (1982) (showerdoor glass).) As Justice Holmes classic statement expresses it, "What usually is done may be evidence of what ought to be done, but what ought to be done is fixed by a standard of reasonable prudence, whether it is complied with or not."

Person of below average intelligence

A person of substandard intelligence is held under common law to the same standard of a reasonable prudent person, to encourage them to exert an increased effort of responsibility to their community, in light of their handicap, and as a result of the practical difficulty of proving what reduced standard should apply (*Vaughn v. Menlove*, 3 Bing. (N.C.) 468, 432 Eng.Rep.490 (1837).) Restatement (Second) of Torts, § 289 cmt. n (noting that the "reasonable person" standard makes allowances for age and physical disability but not "attention, perception, memory, knowledge of other pertinent matters, intelligence, and judgment. Oliver Wendell Holmes, The Common Law, 108 (Little, Brown, & Co. 1881): "The standards of the law are standards of general application. The law takes no account of the infinite varieties of temperament, intellect, and education which make the internal character of a given act so different in different men."

Attorney

An attorney is held to the standard that any reasonable attorney in possession of the same knowledge and skill that an ordinary member of his or her profession possesses, as long as he is acting with reasonable care and diligence, in good faith and honest belief that his advice and acts are well founded at the time. Here, mere error in judgment are excusable (Best Judgment Rule) and cannot be judged solely with the gift of hindsight without substantial injustice. He or she is required to exercise ordinary care and caution (diligence) in the use of that skill (Due Care Rule), and procedural and technical failures are held to be the most common breaches. (cf, *Hodges v. Carter*, 239 N.C. 517, 80 S.E.2d 144 (1954). (failed service of process).)

Person subjected to unexpected danger

In *Cordas v. Peerless Taxi Company*, 27 N.Y.S.2d 198 (1941), Justice Carlin colorfully held that a taxicab driver hijacked at gunpoint by a fleeing mugger in New York City may be excused from negligence for jumping out of the moving taxicab to save his own life, leaving the cab on an unguided trajectory towards bystanders. While some persons might choose to be singularly heroic, that standard is not one that is required for an ordinary prudent person. Such a person is held excused from liability, even if such failure might endanger others. An ordinary prudent person is not under any obligation to undertake a heroic duty at the risk of his own life. "The first duty in an emergency is to one's own self, as long as that person did not contribute to or cause the emergency." (Emergency Doctrine.)

Negligence *per se*

When a state criminal statute is violated in the course of performing an assertedly negligent act, under certain circumstances a court may adopt the statute as establishing a standard of care for tortious liability as well. This is negligence *per se*. It follows the reasoning that if a legislature reached findings of public interest in enacting the statute, these same considerations could arguably apply in cases of negligence. There is no negligence *per se* doctrine in federal law.

Four elements are deemed necessary for a statute to apply in a negligence case. First the person harmed must be a member of the class of persons which the law was intended to protect. Second, the danger or harm must be one that the law was intended to prevent. Thirdly, there must be some causal relationship established between the breach of the statute and the harm caused. Fourthly, the criminal statute must be concrete, specific and measurable enough to clearly establish a standard of breach. Courts are reluctant to create new torts out of criminal statutes. (See Restatement (Second) of Torts, sections 297, 288.)

However, there are five valid excuses that are available for a defendant to defeat a standard of negligence *per se*. (Restatement (Second) of Torts section 288.1(2).) First, the defendant may not know of the breach due to incompetence. Secondly, he might either lack knowledge or reason to know of the breach or duty. Furthermore, for some explainable reason, he may be unable to comply, despite diligence. The breach may be due to a sudden emergency not of one's own making. And lastly, in special situations it may be safer to not comply than to comply. In cases where these defenses are applied, negligence *per se* doctrine creates no more than a rebuttable presumption of negligence that shifts the burden of proof from the plaintiff to the defendant.

Reasonable Person/Ordinary Care

In balancing risks to establish a reasonable person's standard of ordinary care, the rule has been established that the probability of the harm potentially caused (P) must be balanced along with the gravity of the harm which could result (G), against the burden of conforming to a new and less dangerous course of action (B) along with the utility of maintaining the same course of action as it was (U). This is sometimes noted in shorthand as P+G v. B+U, deriving from a formulation expressed by Judge Learned Hand. (*United States v. Carroll Towing Co.*, 159 F.2d 169 (1947).)

See also

- National Care Standards (Scotland)
- Care Standards Act 2000
- Standard of care in English law
- General Social Care Council
- Duty of care
- Reasonable person

References

Duty of care in English law

In English tort law, an individual may owe a **duty of care** by another, to ensure that they do not suffer any unreasonable harm or loss. If such a duty is found to be breached, a legal liability is imposed upon the tortfeasor to compensate the victim for any losses they incur. The idea of individuals owing strangers a duty of care – where beforehand such duties were only found from contractual arrangements – developed at common law, throughout the 20th century. The doctrine was significantly developed in the case of *Donoghue v Stevenson*,[1] where a woman succeeded in establishing a manufacturer of ginger beer owed her a duty of care, where it had been negligently produced. Following this, the duty concept has expanded into a coherent judicial test, which must be satisfied in order to claim in negligence.

Generally, a duty of care arises where one individual or group undertakes an activity which could reasonably harm another, either physically, mentally, or economically. This includes common activities such as driving (where physical injury may occur), as well as specialised activities such as dispensing reliant economic advice (where economic loss may occur). Where an individual has not created a situation which may cause harm, no duty of care exists to warn others of dangerous situations or prevent harm occurring to them; such acts are known as pure omissions, and liability may only arise where a prior special relationship exists to necessitate them.

Duty of Care

The first element of negligence is the legal duty of care. This concerns the relationship between the defendant and the claimant, which must be such that there is an obligation upon the defendant to take proper care to avoid causing injury to the plaintiff in all the circumstances of the case. There are two ways in which a duty of care may be established:

1. the defendant and claimant are within one of the 'special relationship'; or
2. outside of these relationships, according to the principles developed by case law.

The principles delineated in Caparo V Dickman specify a tripartite test:

1. Was the harm reasonably foreseeable?
2. Was there a requisite degree of proximity between the claimant and the defendant
3. Is it fair, just and resonable to impose a duty of care; are there precluding public policy concerns?

There are a number of distinct and recognisable situations in which the courts recognise the existence of a duty of care. Examples include

- one road-user to another
- employer to employee
- manufacturer to consumer
- doctor to patient
- solicitor to client

The neighbour principle

The common law position regarding negiligence recognised strict categories of negligence. This position was significantly changed in the case of *Donoghue v Stevenson*, in 1932, which established that a duty of care applied despite no prior relationship or interaction and was not constrained by privity of contract.[2] Here, a duty of care was found to be owed by a manufacturer to an end consumer, for negligence in the production of his goods. Mrs Donoghue's claim for damages for gastroenteritis and nervous shock were allowed, where a ginger beer manufacturer had negligently allowed a snail into a bottle, which she had consumed. Lord Atkin established liability on the basis that a neighbour principle existed between the two parties, to ensure reasonable care was taken in the production of the ginger beer, so as not to cause Mrs Donoghue any unreasonable harm:

> There must be, and is, some general conception of relations giving rise to a duty of care, of which the particular cases found in the books are but instances. ... The rule that you are to love your neighbour becomes in law you must not injure your neighbour; and the lawyer's question: Who is my neighbour? receives a restricted reply. You must take reasonable care to avoid acts or omissions which you can reasonably foresee would be likely to injure your neighbour. Who, then, in law, is my neighbour? The answer seems to be - persons who are so closely and directly affected by my act that I ought reasonably to have them in contemplation as being so affected when I am directing my mind to the acts or omissions that are called in question.[3]

Lord Atkin's speech established a **neighbour principle,**[4] or a general duty that individuals must take reasonable care in their actions or omissions, so as not to cause harm to others proximate to them. It did not matter that Mrs Donoghue was unidentified or unknown to the manufacturer; as the type of harm which occurred was foreseeable through the negligence of the ginger beer manufacturer.[4]

The Anns test

Following the firm establishment of the neighbour principle in negligence, it became clear in subsequent years that it did not represent an easily applicable approach to new forms of duty, or to unprecedented situations of negligence.[5] As such, new categories of negligence evolved, as in Hedley Byrne & Co Ltd v Heller & Partners Ltd,[6] to cover different types of negligent acts, rather than a coherent doctrine or ratio being taken from *Donoghue v Stevenson.*[7] Some thirty years after Donoghue was decided, in *Home Office v Dorset Yacht Co Ltd,*[8] Lord Reid stated judicially that: "the time has come when we can and should say that it ought to apply unless there is some justification or valid explanation for its exclusion."[9] It was not until the case of *Anns v Merton London Borough Council*[10] however, that the neighbour principle was adopted in a formal test for negligence. The case involved the negligent construction of a block of maisonettes, commissioned by the Merton London Borough Council. The flats, finished in 1972, had poorly constructed foundations, resulting in sloping of floors, and cracks in the walls. The lessees of the maisonettes sued the council in negligence, alleging a duty of care existed for the building to be properly constructed and in a usable state.

In rejecting the previous evolution of duty of care, a categorical approach where a claim would have to fit under previous situations a duty had been found, the House of Lords unanimously found a duty to exist. The test established by Lord Wilberforce – known as the **Anns test** – imposed a prima facie duty of care where:

- A sufficient relationship of proximity or neighbourhood exists between the alleged wrongdoer and the person who has suffered damage, such that carelessness on the part of the former is likely to cause damage to the latter;[11]
- There are no considerations relevant which may reduce or limit the scope of any imposed duty.[12]

The three stage test

Following the establishment of the two stage test for a duty of care, there was a marked judicial retreat from the test, which was widely seen as being too inclusive, and being too easily applicable to cases which might be contrary to public policy.[13] The test was formally overruled in *Murphy v Brentwood District Council,*[14] where the House of Lords invoked the Practice Statement to depart from the Anns test. The resultant test for a duty of care - which remains good law today - can be found in the judgments of *Caparo Industries plc v Dickman.*[15] A large criticism of the Anns test had been that it combined the test for proximity of relationship with foreseeability of harm.[16] Whereas Lord Atkin's neighbour principle emphasised a need for both a proximate relationship, as well as a foreseeability of harm, the Anns test did not make such a clear distinction. Richard Kidner has stated that this led the courts to sometimes ignore relevant policy considerations,[17] and to encourage "lazy thinking and woolly analysis."[18] The resounding test attempts to reconcile the need for a control device, proximity of relationship, with foreseeability of harm. Lord Oliver's speech in *Caparo Industries plc v Dickman* surmises the test for a duty of care:[19]

- The harm which occurred must be a reasonable foreseeable result of the defendant's conduct;
- A sufficient relationship of proximity or neighbourhood exists between the alleged wrongdoer and the person who has suffered damage;

- It is fair, just and reasonable to impose liability.

In reintroducing the need for proximity as a central control device, it has been stated that these three stages are 'ingredients' of liability, rather than tests in their own right.[20] For example, liability can arise between complete strangers, where positive acts involving foreseeable physical harm occur; where negligent omissions and misstatements occur however, it is necessary to show a proximate relationship, as well as a foreseeability of harm.[21]

Status of the claimant

The status of the claimant in an act of negligence can result in a duty of care arising where it would not normally – as is the case with rescuers – or prevent a duty of care existing altogether. Claims that a doctor may owe a mother a duty of care to advise against child birth, and claims that police may owe an individual involved in criminal behavior a duty of care, have been barred. In *McKay v Essex Area Health Authority*,[22] a child's claim that a doctor should have advised his mother to seek an abortion was struck out; Whilst the Congenital Disabilities (Civil Liability) Act allows a course of action where negligence is the cause of a disability, wrongful life has remained barred for policy reasons.[23] Similarly, where a criminal attempted to escape police capture in *Vellino v Chief Constable of the Greater Manchester Police*,[24] his claim that they owed him a duty of care not to let him escape after they had arrested him was branded 'absurd'.[25]

Rescuers

"Danger invites rescue. The cry of distress is the summons to relief. The law does not ignore these reactions of the mind in tracing conduct to its consequences. It recognises them as normal. It places their efforts within the range of the natural and probable. The wrong that imperils life is a wrong to the imperilled victim; it is a wrong also to his rescuer."[26]
Cardozo J, *Wagner v International Railway Co* (1921) 133 NE 437, 232 NY 176

It has been established at common law that those who attempt rescue are owed a duty of care by those who create dangerous situations, in which it is foreseeable rescuers may intervene.[27] This duty can apply to professional rescuers – such as doctors or lifeguards – as much as ordinary individuals,[27] and may even apply where the rescuer engages in a careless or reckless rescue attempt.[28] The basis for this liability was first recognised in *Haynes v Harwood*.[29] Here, a child who threw a stone at a horse, causing it to bolt, was liable to a policeman who attempted to stop it subsequently, and was injured. The duty was confirmed in the later case of *Baker v T E Hopkins & Son Ltd*,[30] with Wilmer LJ stating that:

> Assuming the rescuer not to have acted unreasonably, therefore, it seems to me that he must normally belong to the class of persons who ought to be within the contemplation of the wrongdoer as being closely and directly affected by the latter's act.[31]

The duty of care owed to a rescuer is separate from that owed to those he is rescuing.[27] Where individuals trespassed onto a railway line, putting themselves in danger, they were not owed a duty of care; however, the stationmaster who attempted rescue and was fatally injured was owed a duty of care, as it was foreseeable he would attempt a rescue.[32] Equally, a duty of care may arise where an individual imperils himself, and a rescuer is injured, despite the individual clearly owing himself no duty of care.[33]

Duty of care for omissions

"One can put the matter in political moral or economic terms. In political terms it is less of an invasion of an individual's freedom for the law to require him to consider the safety of others in his actions than to impose upon him a duty to rescue or protect. A moral version of this point may be called the 'Why pick on me?' argument."[34]
Lord Hoffmann, *Stovin v Wise* [1996] AC 923

Generally, no duty of care may arise in relation to pure omissions; acts which if taken would minimise or prevent harm to another individual.[35] However, where an individual creates a dangerous situation - even if blamelessly - a duty of care may arise to protect others from being harmed. Where an individual left his car without lights on at the side of a carriageway, he owed a duty of care to other drivers, despite the road being well lit, and was thus jointly liable when another driver collided with his car.[36]

There are however certain circumstances in which an individual may be liable for omissions, where a prior special relationship exists. Such a relationship may be imposed by statute; the Occupiers' Liability acts for example impose a duty of care upon occupiers of land and properties to protect – in as far as is reasonable – others from harm. In other cases, a relationship may be inferred or imposed based on the need to protect an individual from third parties. In *Stansbie v Troman*[37] a decorator failed to secure a household he was decorating, resulting in a burglary while he was absent; it was found he owed a duty to the household owner to adequately secure the premises in his absence.[38] An authority or service may equally owe a duty of care to individuals to protect them from harm.[39] In *Reeves v Commissioner of Police of the Metropolis*,[40] the police were found to have owed a duty to a prisoner – who was known to be a suicide risk – to ensure he did not commit suicide in their custody.[39] Authorities have also been found liable for failing to protect against the risks of third parties, in certain circumstances. An education authority was found to owe a duty of care to motorists to protect against the risk of a young children in a public road; a driver was injured when forced to swerve, after a four year old child escaped and ran into the path of oncoming traffic.[41]

A duty of care will also apply to an omission if a dangerous act was committed by a third party on the defendant's property which he knew about or should have known about, and he did not take reasonable steps to avert damage to neighbouring properties.

Special types of harm

Psychiatric harm

The duty of care owed to protect others from psychiatric harm is different to that owed for physical harm, with additional control devices and distinctions present in order to limit liability.[42] A successful claim for psychiatric harm must result from a sudden shock (caused by a traumatising event),[42] and the victim must be of ordinary fortitude and mental strength, and not especially susceptible to the harm in question.[43] Whilst a prima facie duty of care is imposed for physical harm where the criteria of proximity, foreseeability, and policy are fulfilled, liability for psychiatric harm rests upon an individual's connection to a traumatising event; those not physically endangered may not be owed a duty of care unless they can fulfill several relational criteria.[44]

The decision of *Page v Smith*[45] establishes liability for psychiatric harm where an individual is endangered physically. Victims in this category are known as primary victims, and are automatically owed a duty of care, as explained by Lord Lloyd:

> Once it is established that the defendant is under a duty of care to avoid causing personal injury to the plaintiff, it matters not whether the injury in fact sustained is physical, psychiatric or both.[46]

Further individuals are classed as secondary victims, and must meet several criteria in order to establish a duty of care is owed to them. There are several types of victims whom the court have recognised; employees who suffer excessive stress at work,[47] individuals witnessing the destruction of their property,[48] while those witnessing especially traumatising scenes involving others are secondary victims.[49] Case law surrounding psychiatric harm focuses primarily on secondary victims; recovery for witnessing the injury and harm of others has been limited primarily by the decision of *Alcock v Chief Constable of South Yorkshire*,[50] which establishes several boundaries and criteria for imposing liability. There must be a close tie of 'love and affection' between the primary victim, and the secondary victim witnessing the traumatic event.[51] Additionally, the cause of the harm must be close and proximate to the shocking event in question, and it must be witnessed by the means of the victim's senses, and not via some form of communication.[52]

Pure economic loss

Negligence which causes no physical or psychiatric harm, but causes economic loss to an individual or organisation, is termed pure economic loss. The idea that a duty of care may be owed to protect against the economic loss of others has been seen as problematic,[53] as the bounds of such liability are potentially unforeseeable, and difficult to establish.[54] Thus, there are several limits in place on the recovery of pure economic loss, with some categories of economic loss being totally unrecoverable altogether. Those affected by damage caused to the property of another company or individual, or who suffer loss due to the purchase of a defective product, for example, cannot ordinarily recover any losses incurred as a result.[55] Instances where a duty of care is recognised generally involve the negligent performance of a service, or the negligent misstatements of professionals, which are then relied upon by others.

The development of pure economic loss stems from the case of *Hedley Byrne & Co Ltd v Heller & Partners Ltd*,[6] where it was first recognised that a duty of care may arise not to cause economic loss to others through negligent misstatements.[56] In this case, Hedley Byrne, an advertising agency, approached Heller & Partners for a credit check on a third company, Easipower Ltd, before carrying out advertising orders on their behalf. Heller & Partners reported that Easipower Ltd was credit-worthy, and in reliance on this statement, Hedley Byrne placed advertising orders for them.[57] When subsequently Easipower Ltd was declared bankrupt, Hedley Byrne took legal action against Heller & Partners, alleging they had been owed a duty of care when consulting for a credit reference. Whilst Hedley Byrne did not succeed in their claim,[58] the House of Lords recognised that such a duty may be owed, where a relationship of reliance exists between two parties.[57]

Liability of public bodies

An organisation or public body may be found to have committed a negligent act in the same way that an individual may; however, for policy reasons, the duty of care which a public body may owe is different to that of private individuals or organisations.[59] Generally, it is where the type of harm involved is not of a physical kind, or a negligent omission is committed, that the formulation of a duty of care differs.

See also

- English tort law
- *Bhamra v Dubb* [2010] EWCA Civ 13 [60]

References

[1] Donoghue v Stevenson (1932) AC 562
[2] Elliott, Quinn, p. 17
[3] [1932] AC 562, at 580
[4] McBride, Bagshaw, p. 72
[5] Elliott, Quinn, p. 18
[6] *Hedley Byrne & Co Ltd v Heller & Partners Ltd* [1964] AC 465
[7] Markesinis, Johnston, Deakin, p. 125
[8] *Home Office v Dorset Yacht Co Ltd* [1970] AC 1004
[9] [1970] AC 1004, at 1027
[10] *Anns v Merton London Borough Council* [1978] AC 728
[11] [1978] AC 728, p. 751
[12] [1978] AC 728, p. 752
[13] McBride, Bagshaw, p. 57
[14] *Murphy v Brentwood District Council* [1991] 1 AC 398
[15] *Caparo Industries plc v Dickman* [1990] 2 AC 605
[16] Steele, p. 146
[17] Kidner, p. 323
[18] Kidner, p. 322
[19] [1990] 2 AC 605, at 632-633
[20] Steele, p. 157
[21] Markesinis, Johnston, Deakin, p. 129
[22] *McKay v Essex Area Health Authority* [1982] QB 1166
[23] Markesinis, Johnston, Deakin, p. 218
[24] *Vellino v Chief Constable of the Greater Manchester Police* [2002] 1 WLR 218
[25] per Schiemann LJ, [2002] 1 WLR 218, at 19
[26] (1921) 133 NE 437, 232 NY 176 at 180
[27] Markesinis, Johnston, Deakin, p. 219
[28] Steele, p. 202
[29] *Haynes v Harwood* [1935] 1 KB 146
[30] *Baker v T E Hopkins & Son Ltd* [1959] 1 WLR 966
[31] [1959] 1 WLR 966, at 981
[32] [1963] 2 QB 650, at 651
[33] Cooke, p. 198
[34] [1996] AC 923, pp. 943-944
[35] per Lord Goff in *Smith v Littlewoods*: "the common law does not impose liability for what are called pure omissions" [1987] 2 AC 241 at 247
[36] See synopsis of: *Lee v Lever* [1974] RTR 35, p. 35
[37] *Stansbie v Troman* [1948] 2 KB 48
[38] McBride, Bagshaw, p. 553
[39] McBride, Bagshaw, p. 552
[40] *Reeves v Commissioner of Police of the Metropolis*
[41] Steele, p. 166
[42] Steele, p. 302
[43] Steele, p. 303
[44] Elliott, Quinn, p. 39
[45] Page v Smith [1996] AC 155
[46] [1996] AC 155, at 190
[47] Recognised as primary victims in *Walker v Northumberland County Council* [1995] 1 All ER 737
[48] Recognised possibly as primary victims since the Alcock criteria were not applied in *Attia v British Gas plc* [1988] QB 304
[49] Steele, p. 317
[50] *Alcock v Chief Constable of South Yorkshire* [1992] 1 AC 310
[51] Nolan, p. 7
[52] Nolan, p. 8
[53] Steele, p. 339
[54] Elliott, Quinn, p. 25
[55] Steele, p. 341
[56] Elliott, Quinn, p. 26

[57] McBride, Bagshaw, p. 125
[58] The House of Lords finding that the disclaimer of the reference (that it had been given "without responsibility") precluded liability.
[59] Markesinis, Deakins, p. 208
[60] http://www.bailii.org/ew/cases/EWCA/Civ/2010/13.html

Bibliography

- Bagshaw, Roderick; McBride, Nicholas (2008). *Tort Law*. Longman. ISBN 1-4058-5949-0.
- Deakin, Simon; Johnston, Angus; Markesinis, Basil (2007). *Markesinis and Deakin's Tort Law*. Oxford University Press. ISBN 0-19-928246-3.
- Elliott, Catherine; Quinn, Frances (2007). *Tort Law*. Longman. ISBN 1-4058-4672-0.
- Kidner, Richard (1987). "Resiling from the Anns principle: the variable nature of proximity in negligence". *Legal Studies* (Blackwell Publishing) **7** (3).
- Donal, Nolan (2004). "Psychiatric injury at the crossroads". *Journal of Personal Injury Law* (1).
- Steele, Jenny (2007). *Tort Law: Text, Cases, & Materials: Text, Cases, and Materials (Paperback)*. Oxford University Press. ISBN 0-19-924885-0.

Breach of duty in English law

In English tort law, there can be no liability in negligence unless the claimant establishes both that they were owed a duty of care by the defendant, and that there has been a **breach of that duty**. The defendant is in breach of duty towards the claimant if their conduct fell short of the standard expected under the circumstances.

General standard of care

In order not to breach a duty of care, a defendant must generally meet the standard of a 'reasonable man' as Baron Alderson stated in *Blyth v Birmingham Waterworks* (1856) 11 Exch 781.[1]

A reasonable person can be defined as 'the man on the Clapham omnibus' as Greer LJ explains in *Hall v Brooklands Auto-Racing Club* (1933) 1 KB 205. Lord Steyn describes the term as 'commuters on the London Underground' (*MacFarlane v. Tayside Health Board* [2] (1999) 3 WLR).

This is an objective standard, based on an average person. It does not require perfection, but takes into account that an average person does not foresee every risk. The average person is not assumed to be flawless, but ordinarily careful and prudent.

Special standards

The standard of "the man on the Clapham omnibus" is not applied in all cases, since this might lead to unfairness. There are defendants for whom this standard is much too low and would exonerate an obvious wrongdoing. In other cases, the standard may be seen as too demanding of the defendant in the circumstances. The most common examples are the cases of specialist defendants, inexperienced defendants and child defendants.

Skilled defendants (specialists)

The test of an ordinary average person would not be appropriate for defendants that profess or hold themselves out as professing a certain skill. The "man on the Clapham omnibus" does not have that skill and the conduct expected from a skilled professional is not the same as could be expected of an ordinary man in the same circumstances.[3] The general standard applied to professionals is therefore that of a "reasonable professional", e.g. car mechanic, doctor etc.

Novices (imperitia culpae adnumerator)

Novices in a certain area of skill must show the same standard of care as a reasonable person with that particular skill. No allowance is given for the defendant's lack of experience.

- *Nettleship v Weston* (1971) 3 All ER 581 requires a novice driver to show the same standard of care as a reasonably competent driver.
- *Wilsher v Essex Area Health Authority* (1986) 3 All ER 801 expects a junior doctor to perform compliant to the standard of a competent and skilled doctor working in the same post.
- *Wells v Cooper* (1958) 2 All ER 527 states that someone who does DIY jobs repairing their own house is expected to show the same standard of care as a reasonably skilled amateur in the particular trade involved. However, they are not required to reach the standard of a professional.

It is important to note that the claimant's knowledge of the defendant's lack of experience in the skill he is exercising does not result in the standard being lowered. In *Nettleship v Weston*, a driving instructor was injured due to a mistake of his student. The student argued that the instructor was aware of her lack of experience, but the Court of Appeal refused to accommodate this fact in their decision on the standard of care expected from her. At the same time, the teacher's award of damages was reduced due to his contributory negligence.

Children

While no allowance is made for novices, the courts are prepared to lower the standard of care expected of children, on account of their age. A child defendant is expected to meet the standard of a reasonable child of the same age.

- *Gough v Thorne* (1966) 3 All ER 398: a 13½ year old girl was not contributorily negligent when she crossed the road without looking after being beckoned by a lorry driver and was hit by a car driving at excessive speed.
- *Mullin v Richards* [1998] 1 All ER 920: a fifteen-year-old girl was not negligent when she was play fighting with a friend and a ruler she was fencing with shattered, a splinter flying into the other girl's eye.

Conduct expected of a reasonable person

In the usual case, having established that there is a duty of care, the claimant must prove that the defendant failed to do what the reasonable person ("reasonable professional", "reasonable child") would have done in the same situation. If the defendant fails to come up to the standard, this will be a breach of the duty of care. This is judged by reference to the following factors:

- What did the defendant know? According to Denning LJ. in *Roe v Minister of Health* (1954) 2 AER 131, the defendant will only be liable if the reasonable person would have foreseen the loss or damage in the circumstances prevailing at the time of the alleged breach of duty.
- What was the degree of risk? The greater the risk that serious harm can be inflicted, the greater the precautions that the defendant will be required to take. In *Bolton v Stone*[1951] A.C. 850, [1951] 1 All E.R. 1078, a cricket club was not negligent when a ball was hit out of the ground and injured the plaintiff, because the likelihood of this occurring was so small that the defendant could not be expected to have taken precautions. In *Miller v. Jackson* ([1977] QB 966, [1977] 3 WLR 20, [1977] 3 All ER 338 however, the ball was hit out of the ground several times every season. In these circumstances, the club was expected to take precautions.
- How practical were these precautions? In *Wilson v Governor of Sacred Heart Roman Catholic Primary School* (1997) EWCA Civ 2644 it was held that a primary school was not negligent in not employing someone to supervise the playground after the close of school hours and until all the children had left. In *Haley v London Electricity Board* [1964] 3 All ER 185, a blind man fell into a hole in the ground that was indicated by a visual sign. He became deaf as a result. It was held that it was foreseeable that a blind man would be walking on the street and the risk of him injuring himself justified the precautions of putting up a barrier. The test is a balance of reasonableness of precautions against the likelihood of injury being sustained.

- What is the social importance of the defendant's activity? If the defendant's actions serve a socially useful purpose then they may have been justified in taking greater risks. Thus, in *Watt v Hertfordshire CC* (1954) 2 AER 368, the fire brigade was not negligent in getting the wrong vehicle to the scene of an accident because valuable time would have been lost in getting the best vehicle there to help. Since 26 July 2006, this consideration has had a statutory basis under section 1 of the Compensation Act 2006.
- Common practice. A defendant complying with a common practice in his area of activity will usually be considered to have met the standard of a reasonable man, unless the court judges the practice itself to be negligent. In *Paris v Stepney Borough Council* (1951) 1 AER 42 although there was a practice of not providing employees with safety goggles, the Council owed a special duty to protect the claimant because he had already lost the sight of one eye.

Sporting events

The conduct expected from a participant in a sports event towards his competitors or spectators differs from the conduct of a reasonable person outside such events. It has been held that in the "heat and flurry" of a competition, a participant will only be in breach of duty towards other participants and spectators if he shows "reckless disregard for their safety".[4] At the same time, in another case,[5] the standard of care expected from one player towards another is the usual standard of taking "all reasonable care in the circumstances in which they were placed", although in that case the defendant was also found to be acting recklessly. It is not clear at present if and how the two approaches can be reconciled.

Burden of proof

Whether or not the defendant in a given case has conducted himself below the standard of "a reasonable person" is a question of fact and it is for the claimant to prove this fact. However, in certain situations it is unlikely that a certain event could take place without the defendant's negligence, for example if a surgeon left a scalpel in the patient's body. In such cases, it is said that "the thing speaks for itself" (*res ipsa loquitur*), and it is for the defendant to show that the fact causing the damage was not attributable to his negligence.

The claimant may raise res ipsa loquitur to shift the evidential burden to the defendant. To do so, following criteria must be satisfied:

1. The incident occurred in an unexplainable fashion;
2. The incident would not have occurred in the ordinary course of events if not defendant's negligence; and
3. The defendant or defendants had control of the injury causing object.

See also

- Damages
- Bolam Test

Notes

[1] "Negligence is the omission to do something that a reasonable man, guided upon those considerations which ordinarily regulate the conduct of human affairs, would do, or doing something that a prudent and reasonable man would not do."

[2] http://www.bailii.org/uk/cases/UKHL/1999/50.html

[3] See *Bolam v. Friern Hospital Management Committee* [1957] 2 All ER 118

[4] See *Wooldridge v Sumner* [1963] 2 QB 23 regarding the spectators, and *Harrison v Vincent* [1982] RTR 8 regarding other sportsmen

[5] See *Condon v Basi* [1985] 2 All ER 453

References

- Alan Miller & Ronen Perry, The Reasonable Person (http://ssrn.com/abstract=1883208), New York University Law Review
- Wenham, David. (1998). "Negligent Children". 4 *WebJCLI* (http://webjcli.ncl.ac.uk/1998/issue4/wenham4.html)

Reasonable person

The **reasonable person** (historically *reasonable man*) is one of many tools for explaining the law to a jury.[1] The "reasonable person" is an emergent concept of common law.[2] While there is (loose) consensus in black letter law, there is no universally accepted, technical definition. As a legal fiction,[2] the "reasonable person" is not an average person or a typical person. Instead, the "reasonable person" is a composite of a relevant community's judgment as to how a typical member of said community should behave in situations that might pose a threat of harm (through action or inaction) to the public.[3]

The standard also holds that each person owes a duty to behave as a reasonable person would under the same or similar circumstances.[4] [5] While the specific circumstances of each case will require varying kinds of conduct and degrees of care, the reasonable person standard undergoes no variation itself.[6] [7]

The "reasonable person" construct can be found applied in many areas of the law. The standard performs a crucial role in determining negligence in both criminal law—that is, criminal negligence—and tort law.

The standard also has a presence in contract law, though its use there is substantially different.[8] It is used to determine contractual intent, or if a breach of the standard of care has occurred, provided a duty of care can be proven. The intent of a party can be determined by examining the understanding of a reasonable person, after consideration is given to all relevant circumstances of the case including the negotiations, any practices the parties have established between themselves, usages and any subsequent conduct of the parties.[9]

The standard does not exist independently of other circumstances within a case that could affect an individual's judgment.

History

In 1835, Adolphe Quetelet's detailed the characteristics of l'homme moyen. His work translates into English several ways. As a result, some authors pick "average man", "common man", "reasonable man", or give up and stick to "l'homme moyen". Quetelet was a Belgian astronomer, mathematician, statistician and sociologist. He documented the physical characteristics of man on a statistical basis and discussed man's motivations when acting in society.[10]

At the age of two, the "reasonable person" made his first appearance in the English case of *Vaughan v. Menlove* (1837).[11] In *Menlove*, the defendant had stacked hay on his rental property in a manner prone to spontaneous ignition. After he had been repeatedly warned over the course of five weeks, the hay ignited and burned the defendant's barns and stable, and then spread to the landlord's two cottages on the adjacent property. Menlove's attorney admitted his client's "misfortune of not possessing the highest order of intelligence," arguing that negligence should only be found if the jury decided Menlove had not acted with "*bona fide* [and] to the best of his [own] judgment."

The *Menlove* court disagreed, reasoning that such a standard would be too subjective, instead preferring to set an objective standard for adjudicating cases:

> The care taken by a prudent man has always been the rule laid down; and as to the supposed difficulty of applying it, a jury has always been able to say, whether, taking that rule as their guide, there has been negligence on the occasion in question. Instead, therefore, of saying that the liability for negligence should be

> co-extensive with the judgment of each individual, which would be as variable as the length of the foot of each individual, we ought rather to adhere to the rule which requires in all cases a regard to caution such as a man of ordinary prudence would observe. That was, in substance, the criterion presented to the jury in this case and, therefore, the present rule must be discharged.

English courts upheld the standard again nearly 20 years later in *Blyth v. Company Proprietors of the Birmingham Water Works,*[12] holding:

> Negligence is the omission to do something which a reasonable man, guided upon those considerations which ordinarily regulate the conduct of human affairs, would do, or doing something which a prudent and reasonable man would not do.

Rationale

American jurist Oliver Wendell Holmes, Jr. explained the theory behind the reasonable person standard as stemming from the impossibility of "measuring a man's powers and limitations."[13] Individual, personal quirks inadvertently injuring the persons or property of others are no less damaging than intentional acts. For society to function, "a certain average of conduct, a sacrifice of individual peculiarities going beyond a certain point, is necessary to the general welfare."[13] Thus, a reasonable application of the law is sought, compatible with planning, working, or getting along with others. As such, "his neighbors accordingly require him, at his proper peril, to come up to their standard, and the courts which they establish decline to take his personal equation into account."[13]

The reasonable person standard is by no means democratic in its scope; it is, contrary to popular conception, intentionally distinct from that of the "average person," who is not necessarily guaranteed to always be reasonable.[14] The reasonable person will weigh all of the following factors before acting:

- the foreseeable risk of harm his actions create versus the utility of his actions;
- the extent of the risk so created;
- the likelihood such risk will actually cause harm to others;
- any alternatives of lesser risk, and the costs of those alternatives.

Taking such actions requires the reasonable person to be appropriately informed, capable, aware of the law, and fair-minded. Such a person might do something extraordinary in certain circumstances, but whatever that person does or thinks, it is always reasonable.

The reasonable person has been called an "excellent but odious character."[15]

> He is an ideal, a standard, the embodiment of all those qualities which we demand of the good citizen ... [he] invariably looks where he is going, ... is careful to examine the immediate foreground before he executes a leap or bound; ... neither stargazes nor is lost in meditation when approaching trapdoors or the margins of a dock; ... never mounts a moving [bus] and does not alight from any car while the train is in motion, ... uses nothing except in moderation, and even flogs his child in meditating only on the golden mean.[16]

English legal scholar Percy Henry Winfield summarized much of the literature by observing that:

> [H]e has not the courage of Achilles, the wisdom of Ulysses or the strength of Hercules, nor has he the prophetic vision of a clairvoyant. He will not anticipate folly in all its forms but he never puts out of consideration the teachings of experience shows such negligence and so will guard against negligence of others when experience shows such negligence to be common. He is a reasonable man but not a perfect citizen, nor a "paragon of circumspection. ..."[17]

Hand Rule

Under American common law, a well known—though nonbinding—test for determining how a reasonable person might weigh the criteria listed above was set down in *United States v. Carroll Towing Co.*[18] by the Chief Justice of the Second Circuit Court, Learned Hand. The case concerned a barge that had broken her mooring with the dock. Writing for the court, Hand held:

> [T]he owner's duty, as in other similar situations, to provide against resulting injuries is a function of three variables: (1) The probability that she will break away; (2) the gravity of the resulting injury, if she does; (3) the burden of adequate precautions.

While the test offered by Hand does not encompass all the criteria available above, juries in a negligence case might well still be instructed to take the other factors into consideration in determining whether the defendant was negligent.[19]

Personal circumstances

While the legal fiction[2] of the reasonable person represents the ideal human actor, one would be hard pressed to characterize any individual human as meeting the standard, whether in whole or in part, all of the time. Since some human actors have limitations, the standard only requires that people act similarly to how "a reasonable person under the circumstance" would, as if their limitations were themselves circumstances. As such, courts require that the reasonable person be viewed as experiencing the same limitations as the defendant.

For example, a disabled defendant is held to a standard that, by necessity, represents how a reasonable person with that same disability would act.[20] One should not mistake this allowance for physical limitations as an allowance for poor judgment, attempting acts beyond one's abilities, or acting too quickly, etc. Were such allowances made for every defendant, there would be as many different standards for negligence as there were defendants; and courts would spend innumerable hours, and the parties much more money, on determining that particular defendant's reasonableness, character, and intelligence.

By using the reasonable person standard, the courts instead use an objective tool and avoid such subjective evaluations. The result is a standard that allows the law to behave in a uniform, foreseeable, and neutral manner when attempting to determine liability.

Children

One broad allowance made to the reasonable person standard is for children. The standard here requires that a child act in a similar manner to how a "reasonable person of like age, intelligence, and experience under like circumstances" would act.[21] In many common law systems, children under the age of 6 or 7 are typically exempt from any liability, whether civil or criminal, as they are deemed to be unable to understand the risk involved in their actions. Children of ages 7 to 17 are held to a reasonable person standard that factors in the criteria above. Although these allowances are made for children, they can still act, and are sometimes found to have acted, in a negligent manner.

In some jurisdictions one of the exceptions to these allowances concern children engaged in what is primarily considered to be high-risk adult activity, such as operating a motor vehicle,[22] [23] and in some jurisdictions children can also be "tried as an adult" for serious crimes, such as murder, which causes the court to disregard the defendant's age.

Mentally ill

The reasonable person standard makes no allowance for the mentally ill.[24] Such a refusal goes back to the standard set in *Menlove*, where Menlove's attorney argued for the subjective standard. In the 170 years since, the law has kept to the legal judgment of having only the single, objective standard. Such judicial adherence sends a message that the mentally ill would do better to refrain from taking risk-creating actions, unless they exercise a heightened degree of self-restraint and precaution, if they intend to avoid liability. Generally, the courts have rationed that by not accepting mental illness as a bar to recovery a liable third party, in the form of a care giver, will be more likely to protect the public because of the potential for liability. The courts have also stated that the reasoning behind the harsh treatment is because, unlike children or the physically disabled, members of the public are unable to identify a person with a mental illness.

Professionals

In cases where a human actor utilizes a professional skill set, the "reasonable person under the circumstances" test becomes elevated to a standard of whether the person acted how a "reasonable professional under the circumstances" would have, without regard to whether that actor is actually a professional, and further without regard to the degree of training or experience of that particular actor.[25] Other factors also become relevant, such as the degree to which the professional is educated (i.e., whether a specialist within the specific field, or just a general practitioner of the trade), and customary practices and general procedures of similar professionals.

However, such other relevant factors are never dispositive. Some professions may maintain a custom or practice long after a better method has become available. The new practices, though less risky, may be entirely ignored. In such cases, the practitioner may very well have acted unreasonably despite following custom or general practices.[26]

Medical professionals

In the realm of healthcare, plaintiffs must prove via expert testimony the standard of medical care owed and a departure from that standard. The only exception to the requirement of expert testimony is where the departure from accepted medical practices was so egregious that a layperson can readily recognize the departure.[27]

However, controversial medical practices can be deemed reasonable when followed by a respected and reputable minority of the medical field,[28] or where the medical profession cannot agree over which practices are best.[29]

Armed professionals

The "reasonable officer" standard is a method often applied to law enforcement and other armed professions to help determine if a use of force was correctly applied. The test is usually applied to whether the level of force used was excessive or not. If an appropriately trained professional, knowing what the subject of the investigation knew at the time and following their agency guidelines (such as a force continuum), would have used the same level of force or higher, then the standard is met. If the level of response is determined to be justified, the quantity of force used is usually presumed to have been necessary unless there are additional factors. For example, should it be determined that a trained police officer was justified in using deadly force against a suspect, the number of times he fired is presumed to have been necessary to stop the suspect's action that justified use of deadly force, as long as there aren't other factors such as a reckless disregard of other officers' or bystanders' safety, or it is clearly proven that additional force was used after the suspect was no longer a threat.

Inexperience

When any person undertakes a skills-based activity that creates a risk to others, they are held to the minimum standard of how a reasonable person experienced in that task would act,[30] regardless of their actual level of experience.[23] [31]

External circumstances

Factors external to the defendant are always relevant. Additionally, so is the context within which each action is made. It is within these circumstances that the determinations and actions of the defendant are to be judged. There are myriad factors that could provide inputs into how a person acts: individual perceptions, knowledge, the weather, etc. The standard of care required for each set of circumstances will vary, yet the level of care due is always what is reasonable for that set of circumstances.[32]

While community customs may be relied upon to indicate what kind of action is expected in light of given circumstances, such customary requirements are not themselves conclusive of what a reasonable person would do.[14] [33]

It is precisely for this wide-ranging variety of possible facts that the reasonable person standard is so broad (and often confusing and difficult to apply). However, a few general areas of relevant circumstances rise above the others.

Emergency doctrine

Allowing for circumstances under which a person must act urgently is important to preventing hindsight bias from affecting the trier of fact. Given pressing circumstances, a reasonable person may not always act in a manner similar to how she would have acted in a more relaxed setting. As such, it is only fair that actions be judged in light of any exigent conditions that could have affected how the defendant acted.[34] [35]

Available resources

In certain circumstances, human actors are faced with the problem of making do only with what is available. Such circumstances are relevant to any determination of whether the defendant acted reasonably. Where necessary resources are scarce, certain actions may be reasonable that would be unreasonable if those same resources were available and either readily at hand or realistically obtainable given other circumstances.

Negligence *per se*

Because a reasonable person is objectively presumed to know the law, noncompliance with a local safety statute may also constitute negligence. The related doctrine of negligence *per se* addresses the circumstances under which the law of negligence can become an implied cause of action for breaching a statutory standard of care. Conversely, minimal compliance with a safety statute does not always absolve a defendant if the trier of fact determines that the reasonable person should have taken actions beyond and in excess of what the statute required.[36] However, if the trier of fact finds the statute's standard itself is reasonable and the defendant acted in accordance with what the statute contemplated, the duty of care can be deemed met.[37] [38] [39]

Reasonable bystander

For common law contracts, disputes over contract formation are subjected to what is known as the *objective test of assent* in order to determine whether a contract exists. This standard is also known as the *reasonable bystander*, *reasonable third party*, or *reasonable person in the position of the party*.[40] This is in contrast to the subjective test employed in most civil law jurisdictions. The test stems from attempts to balance the competing interests of the judicial policies of assent and of reliability. The former holds that no person ought to be contractually obligated if they did not consent to such an agreement; the latter holds that if no person can rely on actions or words demonstrating consent, then the whole system of commercial exchange will ultimately collapse.[41]

Prior to the 19th century, courts used a test of subjective evalutation;[41] that is, the trier of fact determined each party's understanding.[42] If both parties were of the same mind and understanding on matters, then assent was manifested and the contract was valid. Between the 19th and 20th centuries, the courts shifted toward the objectivist test, reasoning that subjective testimony was often unreliable and self-serving.[41]

From those opposite principles, modern law has found its way to a rough middle ground, though it still shows a strong bias toward the objective test.[40] Promises and agreements are reached through manifestations of consent, and parties are liable for actions that deliberately manifest such consent; however, evidence of either party's state of mind can be used to determine the context of the manifestation if said evidence is reliable and compatible with the manifestation in question, though such evidence is typically given very little weight.[42]

Another circumstance where the reasonable bystander test is used occurs when one party has inadvertently misstated the terms of the contract, and the other party sues to enforce those terms: if it would have been clear to a reasonable bystander that a mistake had been made, then the contract is voidable by the party who made the error; otherwise, the contact is binding.

Reasonable person standard for victims

Reasonable woman

Sexual harassment

A variant of the reasonable person can be found in sexual harassment law as the *reasonable woman* standard. The variation recognizes a difference between men and women regarding the effect of unwanted interaction with a sexual tone. As women have historically been more vulnerable to rape and sex-related violence than have men, some courts believe that the proper perspective for evaluating a claim of sexual harassment is that of the reasonable woman.

Satire

Though the use of the reasonable woman standard has gained traction in some areas of the law, the standard has not escaped the crosshairs of humorists. In 1924, legal humorist A. P. Herbert considered the concept of the reasonable man at length in the fictional case of "Fardell v. Potts." In Herbert's fictional account, the judge addressed the lack of a reasonable woman standard in the common law, and ultimately concluded that "a reasonable woman does not exist."[43]

L'homme moyen sensuel

The subject of l'homme moyen sensuel doesn't speak of a reasonable person's ability, actions, nor understandings. Rather it refers to an effect that occurs to a reasonable person when presented with some form of information either by image or sound, or upon reading a book or magazine. In 1917, this aspect of the reasonable person was the subject of a poem by Ezra Pound. The best-known use of l'homme moyen sensuel was when Judge Woosley lifted the ban on the book Ulysses by James Joyce. [44] That ruling contemplated the effect the book would have upon a reasonable person of reasonable sensibility. Similarly, the publisher of Howl and Other Poems ended up in court in California charged with publishing an obscene book, and l'homme moyen sensuel played a role in declaring the publisher innocent.[45] It was nearly two decades after Woosley that the US Supreme Court set down the standard by which materials, when viewed by l'homme moyen sensuel, were judged either obscene or not.[46] Generally, it has been l'homme moyen sensuel that has dictated what is and is not obscene or pornographic in books, movies, pictures, and now the Internet for at least the past 100 years.

Qualifications

Very often, for instance, in the case of noise ordinances, the enforcement of the law is only for the purpose of protecting the right of a reasonable person of normal sensitivity.[47] [48] [49]

Equivalents outside of common law systems

In Roman law, the standard of reasonable care, for example by a trustee or guardian, was that of the *pater familias* or the *bonus pater familias* ("good father of a family"). In French law, this is rendered as the *bon père de famille*, an expression also used in Quebec until it was superseded by the common-law influenced *personne raisonnable*. In Portuguese and Portugal-related legal systems, the standard is the *bom pai de família*.

See also

• Beyond a reasonable doubt	• Gender discrimination	• Reasonable suspicion
• Casuistry	• Man on the Bondi tram	• Standard of care in English law
• Contract	• Man on the Clapham omnibus/Man on the Shaukiwan tram	• Torts

References

Notes

[1] *Regina v Smith*, 4 AER 289 (http://www.publications.parliament.uk/pa/ld199900/ldjudgmt/jd000727/smith-1.htm) (2000) ("[sub-citing Camplin and Bedder:] the concept of the "reasonable man" has never been more than a way of explaining the law to a jury; an anthropomorphic image to convey to them, with a suitable degree of vividness, the legal principle that even under provocation, people must conform to an objective standard of behaviour that society is entitled to expect").

[2] *Bedder v Director of Public Prosecutions*, 1 WLR 1119 (1954) ("[where reasonable man is deemed a wholly impersonal fiction to which no special characteristic of the accused should be attributed]").

[3] *R v Camplin*, A.C. 705 (1978) ("[a reasonable man] "means an ordinary person of either sex, not exceptionally excitable or pugnacious, but possessed of such powers of self control as everyone is entitled to expect that his fellow citizens will exercise in society as it is today").

[4] *Brown v. Kendall*, 60 Mass. 292 (1850).

[5] Franklin, at 54

[6] *Triestram v. Way*, 281 N.W. 420 (Mich. 1938).

[7] Franklin, at 55

[8] For the use in transnational contract law: Trans-Lex.org (http://www.trans-lex.org/902000)

[9] Determining the Contractual Intent of Parties under the CISG and Common Law -- A Comparative Analysis, European Journal of Law Reform (Kluwer) Vol. 4, No. 4 (2002) 629-643, by Bruno Zeller, 2002, last updated, June 30, 2006 (http://www.cisg.law.pace.edu/cisg/biblio/zeller8.html#iii)

[10] On Man, and the development of his faculties, The Athenæm, by By A. Quetelet, Secretary to the Royal Academy of Brussels. London: Bossange & Co pp. 593-594, August 8 1835 (http://www.stat.ucla.edu/history/athenaeum.pdf)

[11] *Vaughan v. Menlove*, 132 ER 490 (Common Pleas 1837).

[12] *Blyth v. Company Proprietors of the Birmingham Water Works*, 156 ER 1047 (Exchequer 1856).

[13] Holmes, at 108.

[14] *The T.J. Hooper*, 60 F.2d 737 (2d Cir. 1932).

[15] Herbert, at 12.

[16] Herbert, pp. 9-11.

[17] Business Law of Australia (Vermeesch & Lindgren) 4th Ed, 1983, p 1113

[18] *United States v. Carroll Towing Co.*, 159 F.2d 169 (2d. Cir. 1947).

[19] Glannon, at pg. 74.

[20] *Hill v. Greenwood*, 100 N.W. 522 (Iowa 1904).

[21] Restatement of the Law, Second, Torts. §283A

[22] *Robinson v. Lindsay*, 598 P.2d 392 (Wash. 1979).

[23] *Stevens v. Veenstra*, 226 Mich. App. 441 (1997).

[24] *Breunig v. American Family Insurance Co.*, 173 N.W.2d 619 (Wis. 1970).

[25] *Heath v. Swift Wings, Inc.*, 252 S.E.2d 526 (N.C. 1979).

[26] Bolitho v. City and Hackney Health Authority [1997] 4 All ER 771

[27] *Heimer v. Privratsky*, 434 N.W.2d 357 (N.D. 1989).
[28] *Gala v. Hamilton*, 715 A.2d 1108 (Pa. 1998).
[29] *Furey v. Thomas Jefferson Uni. Hospital*, 472 A.2d 1083 (Pa. 1984).
[30] *Delair v. McAdoo*, 188 A. 181 (Pa. 1936).
[31] *Dellwo v. Pearson*, 107 N.W.2d 859 (Minn. 1961).
[32] *Stewart v. Potts*, 654 A.2d 535 (Pa. 1995).
[33] *Texas & Pacific Railway v. Behymer*, 189 U.S. 468, 470 (1903).
[34] *Rivera v. New York City Transit Authority*, 77 N.Y.2d 332 (1991).
[35] Restatement of the Law, Second, Torts. §296
[36] *Clinkscales v. Carver*, 22 Cal.2d 72 (1934).
[37] *Josephson v. Meyers*, 429 A.2d 877 (Conn. 1980).
[38] *Espinoza v. Elgin, Joliet & Eastern Railway*, 649 N.E.2d 1323 (Ill. 1995).
[39] Restatement of the Law, Second, Torts. §288C
[40] Blum, at pg. 53.
[41] Blum, at pg. 52.
[42] Blum, at pg. 54.
[43] Herbet, Alan Patrick, Sir (1989). *Misleading Cases in the Common Law* (http://books.google.com/?id=-u9qWlotKr4C) (4th ed.). Buffalo: William S. Hein & Co., Inc.. ISBN 978-0-8377-2242-9. .
[44] US District Court S. NY, OPINION A. 110-59, by John M. Woolsey, December 6, 1933 (http://xroads.virginia.edu/~MA04/kane/30scensorship/woosley.htm,)
[45] California v. Ferlinghetti (http://mason.gmu.edu/~kthomps4/363-s02/horn-howl.htm)
[46] A tendency to deprave and corrupt, Washington Law Review Vol.85, No. 2, 2007 (http://lawreview.wustl.edu/inprint/85/2/Gillers.pdf)
[47] Bozeman, Montana Noise Ordinance (http://ftp.bozeman.net/bozeman/government/commission/PDF/ordiances/noise.pdf)
[48] Blooming Grove, NY Noise Ordinance (http://www.bloominggrovepolice.com/Noise Law Page.htm)
[49] Town of Romulus, NY Noise Ordinance (http://www.romulustown.com/ordinances/ORDINANCE REGULATING NOISE.pdf)

Sources

- Blum, Brian A. (2004). *Contracts* (3rd ed.). New York, NY: Aspen Publishers. ISBN 0-7355-2612-5.
- Franklin, Marc A. (2002). *Torts* (23rd ed.). Chicago, IL: The BarBri Group. ISBN 0-7355-6168-0.
- Glannon, Joseph W. (2005). *The Law of Torts* (3rd ed.). New York, NY: Aspen Publishers. ISBN 0-7355-8480-X.
- Herbert, A.P. (1932). *Misleading Cases in the Common Law* (7th ed.).
- Miller, Alan & Perry, Ronen, The Reasonable Person (http://ssrn.com/abstract=1883208), New York University Law Review
- Holmes, Oliver Wendell, Jr. (1909). *The Common Law* (http://books.google.com/?id=xXouAAAAIAAJ&dq=holmes+common+law) (2nd ed.). Little, Brown. ISBN 0-674-14605-0.
- "Reasonable woman" (http://www.answers.com/topic/reasonable-woman). *West's Encyclopedia of American Law*. The Gale Group, Inc.. 1998. Retrieved 1 December 2008.

Causation (law)

Causation is the "causal relationship between conduct and result". That is to say that causation provides a means of connecting conduct with a resulting effect, typically an injury. In criminal law, it is defined as the *actus reus* (an action) from which the specific injury or other effect arose and is combined with *mens rea* (a state of mind) to comprise the elements of guilt. Causation is only applicable where a result has been achieved and therefore is immaterial with regard to inchoate offenses.

Background concepts

Most legal systems are to a greater or lesser extent concerned with the notions of fairness and justice. If a state is going to penalise a person or require that person to pay compensation to another for losses incurred, this imposition of liability will be derived from the idea that those who injure others should take responsibility for their actions. Although some parts of any legal system will have qualities of strict liability, in which the *mens rea* is immaterial to the result and subsequent liability of the actor, most look to establish liability by showing that the defendant was the cause of the particular injury or loss.

Even the youngest children quickly learn that, with varying degrees of probability, consequences flow from physical acts and omissions. The more predictable the outcome, the greater the likelihood that the actor caused the injury or loss intentionally. There are many ways in which the law might capture this simple rule of practical experience: that there is a natural flow to events, that a reasonable man in the same situation would have foreseen this consequence as likely to occur, that the loss flowed naturally from the breach of contractual or tortious duty, etc. However it is phrased, the essence of the degree of fault attributed will lie in the fact that reasonable people try to avoid injuring others so, if harm was foreseeable, there should be liability to the extent that the extent of the harm actually resulting was foreseeable.

The relationship between causation and liability

Causation of an event by itself is not sufficient to create legal liability.

Sometimes causation is one part of a multi-stage test for legal liability. For example for the defendant to be held liable for the tort of negligence, the defendant must have (1) owed the plaintiff a duty of care; (2) breached that duty; (3) by so doing caused damage to the plaintiff; and (4) that damage must not have been too remote. Causation is but one component of the tort.

On other occasions causation is the only requirement for legal liability (other than the fact that the outcome is proscribed). For example in the law of product liability, the fact that the defendant's product caused the plaintiff harm is the only thing that matters. The defendant need not also have been negligent.

On still other occasions, causation is irrelevant to legal liability altogether. For example, under a contract of indemnity insurance, the insurer agrees to indemnify the victim for harm not caused by the insurer, but by other parties.

Because of the difficulty in establishing causation, it is one area of the law where the case law overlaps significantly with general doctrines of analytic philosophy to do with causation. The two subjects have long been somewhat intermingled.

Establishing causation

Where establishing causation is required to establish legal liability, it is usually said that it involves a two-stage inquiry.

The first stage involves establishing 'factual' causation. Did the defendant act in the plaintiff's loss? This must be established before inquiring into legal causation.

The second stage involves establishing 'legal' causation. This is often a question of public policy: is this the sort of situation in which, despite the outcome of the factual enquiry, we might nevertheless release the defendant from liability, or impose liability?

Establishing factual causation

The usual method of establishing factual causation is the but-for test. The but for test inquires 'But for the defendant's act, would the harm have occurred?' A shoots and wounds B. We ask 'But for A's act, would B have been wounded?' The answer is 'No.' So we conclude that A caused the harm to B. The but for test is a test of necessity. It asks was it 'necessary' for the defendant's act to have occurred for the harm to have occurred.

One weakness in the but-for test arises in situations where each of several acts alone are sufficient to cause the harm. For example, if both A and B fire what would alone be fatal shots at C at approximately the same time, and C dies, it becomes impossible to say that but-for A's shot, or but-for B's shot alone, C would have died. Taking the but-for test literally in such a case would seem to make neither A nor B responsible for C's death.

The courts have generally accepted the but for test notwithstanding these weaknesses, qualifying it by saying that causation is to be understood "as the man in the street" would: *Yorkshire Dale Steamship Co v Minister of War Transport* [1942] AC 691 (HL), or by supplementing it with "common sense": (*March v Stramare* (1991) 171 CLR 506 (High Court of Australia).

This dilemma was handled in the United States in *State v. Tally*, 15 So 722, 738 (Ala. 1894), where the court ruled that: "The assistance given ... need not contribute to criminal result in the sense that but for it the result would not have ensued. It is quite sufficient if it facilitated a result that would have transpired without it." Using this logic, A and B are liable in that no matter who was responsible for the fatal shot, the other "facilitated" the criminal act even though his shot was not necessary to deliver the fatal blow.

However, legal scholars have attempted to make further inroads into what explains these difficult cases. Some scholars have proposed a test of sufficiency instead of a test of necessity. H. L. A. Hart and Tony Honoré, and later Richard Wright, have said that something is a cause if it is a 'necessary element of a set of conditions jointly sufficient for the result'. This is known as the NESS test. In the case of the two hunters, the set of conditions required to bring about the result of the victim's injury would include a gunshot to the eye, the victim being in the right place at the right time, gravity, etc. In such a set, either of the hunters' shots would be a member, and hence a cause. This arguably gives us a more theoretically satisfying reason to conclude that something was a cause of something else than by appealing to notions of intuition or common sense.

Hart and Honore, in their famous work *Causation in the Law*, also tackle the problem of 'too many causes'. For them, there are degrees of causal contribution. A member of the NESS set is a "causally relevant condition". This is elevated into a "cause" where it is a deliberate human intervention, or an abnormal act in the context. So, returning to our hunter example, hunter A's grandmother's birth is a causally relevant condition, but not a "cause". On the other hand, hunter A's gunshot, being a deliberate human intervention in the ordinary state of affairs, is elevated to the status of "cause". An intermediate position can be occupied by those who "occasion" harm, such as accomplices. Imagine an accomplice to a murder who drives the principal to the scene of the crime. Clearly the principal's act in committing the murder is a "cause" (on the but for or NESS test). So is the accomplice's act in driving the principal to the scene of the crime. However the causal contribution is not of the same level (and, incidentally, this provides some basis for treating principals and accomplices differently under criminal law). Leon Green and Jane Stapleton are two scholars who take the opposite view. They consider that once something is a "but for" (Green) or NESS (Stapleton) condition, that ends the factual inquiry altogether, and anything further is a question of policy.

Establishing legal causation

Notwithstanding the fact that causation may be established in the above situations, the law often intervenes and says that it will nevertheless not hold the defendant liable because in the circumstances the defendant is not to be understood, in a legal sense, as having caused the loss. In the United States, this is known as the doctrine of proximate cause. The most important doctrine is that of *novus actus interveniens*, which means a 'new intervening act' which may 'cut the chain of causation'.

Proximate cause

The but-for test often gives us the right answer to causal problems, but sometimes not. Two difficulties are immediately obvious. The first is that under the but-for test, almost anything is a cause. But for a tortfeasor's grandmother's birth, the relevant tortious conduct would not have occurred. But for the victim of a crime missing the bus, he or she would not have been at the site of the crime and hence the crime would not have occurred. Yet in these two cases, the grandmother's birth or the victim's missing the bus are not intuitively causes of the resulting harm. This often does not matter in the case where cause is only one element of liability, as the remote actor will most likely not have committed the other elements of the test. The legally liable cause is the one closest to or most proximate to the injury. This is known as the Proximate Cause rule. However, this situation can arise in strict liability situations.

Intervening cause

Imagine the following. A critically injures B. As B is wheeled to an ambulance, she is struck by lightning. She would not have been struck if she had not been injured in the first place. Clearly then, A caused B's whole injury on the 'but for' or NESS test. However, at law, the intervention of a supervening event renders the defendant not liable for the injury caused by the lightning.

The effect of the principle may be stated simply:

> if the new event, whether through human agency or natural causes, does not break the chain, the original actor is liable for all the consequences flowing naturally from the initial circumstances. But if the new act breaks the chain, the liability of the initial actor stops at that point, and the new actor, if human, will be liable for all that flows from his or her contribution.

Note, however, that this does not apply if the Eggshell skull rule is used. For details, see the article on the Eggshell Skull doctrine.

Independent sufficient causes

When two or more negligent parties, where the consequence of their negligence joins together to cause damages, in a circumstance where either one of them alone would have caused it anyway, each is deemed to be an "Independent Sufficient Cause," because each could be deemed a "substantial factor," and both are held legally responsible for the damages. For example, where negligent firestarter A's fire joins with negligent firestarter B's fire to burn down House C, both A and B are held responsible. (e.g., *Anderson v. Minneapolis, St: P. & S. St. R.R. Co.*, 146 Minn. 430, 179 N.W. 45 (1920).) This is an element of Legal Cause.

Summers v. Tice Rule

The other problem is that of overdetermination. Imagine two hunters, A and B, who each negligently fire a shot that takes out C's eye. Each shot on its own would have been sufficient to cause the damage. But for A's shot, would C's eye have been taken out? Yes. The same answer follows in relation to B's shot. But on the but-for test, this leads us to the counterintuitive position that neither shot caused the injury. However, courts have held that in order for each of the defendants to avoid liability for lack of actual cause, it is necessary to hold both of them responsible, See *Summers v. Tice*, 33 Cal.2d 80, 199 P.2d 1 (1948). This is known, simply, as the *Summers v. Tice* Rule.

Concurrent actual causes

Suppose that two actors' negligent acts combine to produce one set of damages, where but for either of their negligent acts, no damage would have occurred at all. This is two negligences contributing to a single cause, as distinguished from two separate negligences contributing to two successive or separate causes. These are "concurrent actual causes". In such cases, courts have held both defendants liable for their negligent acts. Example: A leaves truck parked in the middle of the road at night with its lights off. B fails to notice it in time and plows into it, where it could have been avoided, except for want of negligence, causing damage to both vehicles. Both parties were negligent. (*Hill v. Edmonds*, 26 A.D.2d 554, 270 N.Y.S.2d 1020 (1966).)

Foreseeability

This is usually expressed as a question of 'foreseeability'. An actor is liable for the foreseeable, but not the unforeseeable, consequences of his or her act. For example it is foreseeable that if I shoot someone on a beach and they are immobilized, they may drown in a rising tide rather than from the trauma of the gunshot wound or from loss of blood. However it is not (generally speaking) foreseeable that they will be struck by lightning and killed by that event.

This type of causal foreseeability is to be distinguished from foreseeability of extent or kind of injury, which is a question of remoteness of damage, not causation. For example, if I conduct welding work on a dock that lights an oil slick that destroys a ship a long way down the river, it would be hard to construe my negligence as anything other than causal of the ship's damage. There is no *novus actus interveniens*. However, I may not be held liable if that damage is not of a type foreseeable as arising from my negligence: The Wagon Mound (No 1) [1961] AC 388 (Privy Council). That is a question of public policy, and not one of causation.

Example

An example of how foreseeability does not apply to the extent of an injury is the eggshell skull rule. If Neal punched Matt in the jaw, it is foreseeable that Matt will suffer a bodily injury that he will need to go to the hospital for. However, if his jaw is very weak, and his jaw comes completely off from my punch, then the doctor bills, which would have been about $5,000 for wiring his jaw shut had now become $100,000 for a full-blown jaw re-attachment. Neal would still be liable for the entire $100,000, even though $95,000 of those damages were not reasonably foreseeable.

Other relevant considerations

Because causation in the law is a complex amalgam of fact and policy, other doctrines are also important, such as foreseeability and risk. Particularly in the United States, where the doctrine of 'proximate cause' effectively amalgamates the two stage factual then legal causation inquiry favoured in the English system, one must always be alert to these considerations in assessing the postulated relationship between two events.

Foreseeability tests

Some aspects of the physical world are so inevitable that it is always reasonable to impute knowledge of their incidence. So if A abandons B on a beach, A must be taken to foresee that the tide comes in and goes out. But the mere fact that B subsequently drowns is not enough. A court would have to consider where the body was left and what level of injury A believed that B had suffered. If B was left in a position that any reasonable person would consider safe but a storm surge caused extensive flooding throughout the area, this might be a *novus actus*. That B was further injured by an event within a foreseen class does not of itself require a court to hold that every incident falling within that class is a natural link in the chain. Only those causes that are reasonably foreseeable fit naturally into the chain. So if A had heard a weather forecast predicting a storm, the drowning will be a natural outcome. But if this was an event like a flash flood, an entirely unpredictable event, it will be a *novus actus*.

The question of A's beliefs is no different. If A honestly believes that B is only slightly injured and so could move himself out of danger without difficulty, how fair is it to say that he *ought* to have foreseen? The test is what the reasonable person would have known and foreseen, given what A had done. It is the function of any court to evaluate behaviour. A defendant cannot evade responsibility through a form of wilful blindness. Fault lies not only in what a person actually believes, but also in failing to understand what the vast majority of other people would have understood. Hence, the test is hybrid, looking both at what the defendant actually knew and foresaw (i.e. subjective), and at what the reasonable person would have known (i.e. objective) and then combining the conclusions into a general evaluation of the degree of fault or blameworthiness.

Similarly, in the quantification of damages generally and/or the partitioning of damages between two or more defendants, the extent of the liability to compensate the plaintiff(s) will be determined by what was reasonably foreseeable. So if, for example, the plaintiff unexpectedly contributed to the extent of the loss suffered, that additional element would not be included in the damages award even though the plaintiff would not have had the opportunity to make this mistake had it not been for the defendant's breach. In cases involving the partitioning of damages between multiple defendants, each will be liable to the extent that their contribution foreseeably produced the loss.

Risk

Sometimes the reverse situation to a *novus actus* occurs, i.e. factual causation cannot be proved but the court nevertheless does want to hold the defendant liable. In *Sindell v. Abbott Laboratories*, 607 P.2d 924 (Cal. 1980) the plaintiff's mother consumed diethylstilbestrol as a miscarriage preventative.[1] The medicine, later re-called from the market, caused the defendant to develop a malignant bladder tumor due to its negligent manufacture.[1] However, there were many manufacturers of that drug in the market. The manufacturer of the particular medication that caused the injury could not be ascertained for certain.[2] The court held that the defendant was liable in proportion to its market share.[3] They departed from traditional notions of pure cause and adopted a 'risk based' approach to liability. The defendant was held liable because of the amount of risk it contributed to the occasioning of the harm.[3] Note that a risk theory is not strictly a theory built on notions of cause at all, as, by definition, the person who caused the injury could not be ascertained for certain. However, it does show that legal notions of causation are a complex mixture of factual causes and ideas of public policy relating to the availability of legal remedies. In *R v Miller* [1982] UKHL 6, the House of Lords said that a person who puts a person in a dangerous position, in that case a fire, will be criminally liable if he does not adequately rectify the situation.

Evidence proving causation

To be acceptable, any rule of law must be capable of being applied consistently so a definition of the criteria for this qualitative analysis must be supplied. Let us assume a purely factual analysis as a starting point. A injures B and leaves him lying in the road. C is a driver who fails to see B on the road and by running over him, contributes to the cause of his death. It would be possible to ask for a detailed medical evaluation at a post mortem to determine the initial degree of injury and the extent to which B's life was threatened, followed by a second set of injuries from the collision and their contribution. If the first incident merely damaged B's leg so that he could not move, it is tempting to assert that C's driving must have been the more substantial cause and so represents a *novus actus* breaking the chain. Equally, if B was bleeding to death and the only contribution that the driving made was to break B's arm, the driving is not a *novus actus* and does not break the chain. But this approach ignores the issue of A's foresight.

Roads are, by their nature, used by vehicles and it is clearly foreseeable that a person left lying on the road is at risk of being further injured by an inattentive driver. Hence, if A leaves B on the road with knowledge of that risk and the foreseen event occurs, A remains the more proximate cause. This leaves whether the test of foresight should be subjective, objective or hybrid (i.e. both subjective and objective). Obviously, there is no difficulty in holding A liable if A had actual knowledge of the likelihood that B would be further injured by a driver. The fault which caused the initial injury is compounded by the omission to move B to a safer place or call for assistance. But let us assume that A never adverts to the possibility of further injury. The issue is now the extent to which knowledge may be imputed objectively.

The future?

A difficult issue that has arisen recently is the case where the defendant neither factually causes the harm, nor increases the risk of its occurrence. In *Chester v Afshar* [2004] 4 All ER 587 (HL), a doctor negligently failed to warn a patient of risks inherent in an operation, specifically cauda equina syndrome.[4] The patient had the operation and a risk materialized causing injury.[4] It was found that even if the patient had been warned, the patient would still have undergone the operation, simply at a different time.[5] The risk of the injury would be the same at both times. Accordingly, the doctor neither caused the injury (because but for the failure to warn, the patient would still have gone ahead with the operation), nor increased the risk of its occurrence (because the risk was the same either way). Yet the House of Lords, embracing a more normative approach to causation, still held the doctor liable. Lawyers and philosophers continue to debate whether and how this changes the state of the law.

English criminal case law examples

Novus actus interveniens

- **Victim's contribution** *R v Dear* (1996) CLR 595. Believing that the victim had sexually interfered with his 12 year old daughter, the defendant attacked the victim with a Stanley knife. The defendant argued that the chain of causation had been broken because, two days later, the victim had committed suicide either by reopening his wounds or because he had failed to take steps to staunch the blood flow after the wounds had reopened spontaneously (i.e. the potential suicide constituted a *novus actus interveniens*). It was held that the real question was whether the injuries inflicted by the defendant were an operating and significant cause of or contribution to the death. Distinctions between the victim's mere self-neglect (no break in the chain) and the victim's gross self-neglect (break in the chain) were not helpful. The victim's death resulted from bleeding from the artery severed by the defendant. Whether the resumption or continuation of that bleeding was deliberately caused by the victim, the defendant's conduct remained the operative and significant cause of the victim's death.
- **Third party's inadvertent contribution** *R v Smith* (1959) 2 QB 35 the defendant stabbed his victim twice in a barrack room brawl. Another soldier carried him to the medical centre but dropped him twice. The medical captain was very busy and failed to recognise the extent of the injuries. If the soldier had received proper

treatment, he would have had a good chance of a complete recovery. Smith was convicted of manslaughter because the wound was the "operating and substantial cause of death". In *R v Cheshire* (1991) 3 AER 670, the victim was shot in the leg and stomach. In hospital, he suffered pneumonia and respiratory problems in intensive care so had a tracheotomy. After two months, he died. There was some medical negligence because the tracheotomy had caused a thickening of tissue ultimately causing suffocation. In upholding the conviction for murder, Beldam LJ. laid down the following test:

> Even though negligence in the treatment of the victim was the immediate cause of his death, the jury should not regard it as excluding the responsibility of the accused unless the negligent treatment was so independent of his acts, and in itself so potent in causing death, that they regard the contribution made by his acts as insignificant.

- **Third party's deliberate intervention** *R v Malcherek* (1981) 73 Cr. App. R. 173. The victim was placed on a life support machine and, after determining that she was brain dead, the doctors turned off the machine. The defendant appealed the conviction of murder arguing that the doctors had broken the chain of causation by deliberately switching off the life support machine. It was held that the original wounds were the operating and substantial cause of death, and that a life support machine does no more than hold the effect of the injuries in suspension and when the machine is switched off, the original wounds continue to cause the death no matter how long the victim survives after the machine's disconnection. In *R v Pagett* (1983) 76 Cr. App. R. 279, to resist lawful arrest, the defendant held a girl in front of him as a shield and shot at armed policemen. The police instinctively fired back and killed the girl. The Court of Appeal held that the defendant's act caused the death and that the reasonable actions of a third party acting in self-defence could not be regarded as a *novus actus interveniens* because self-defence is a foreseeable consequence of his action and had not broken the chain of causation.

Foreseeability

- **Victim's conscious actions** *R v. Blaue* (1975) 61 Cr. App. R. 271 is a criminal law application of the "thin skull rule" in criminal law. The defendant visited the home of a Jehovah's Witness and demanded sex. When she refused, he stabbed her four times. At hospital, she refused a blood transfusion which would have saved her life. There was no suggestion that the doctors had acted improperly. Blaue was convicted of manslaughter by an unlawful act, namely wounding with intent. "But for" his actions, she would not have been faced with the choice about treatment and those who use violence on others must take their victims as they find them (albeit that he had known her religion and so her refusal was foreseeable).

Causation: law and science compared

Science and law have different functions but share striking similarities. Both purport to provide rational, reasoned, independent, unbiased processes concerned with the objective assessment of evidence. There are also striking differences. Scientific assertions compared with determinations of legal causation have the following characteristics:

- they are population-based, not individual; general not particular;
- they are probabilistic, not deterministic;
- they are generally expressed as the refutation of the hypothesis and not a finding of fact or proof of an allegation;
- the evidence is not exhaustive, whereas an adjudication is determined according to the evidence available.
- science is not as concerned with finality as is law. There is no *res judicata* or *collateral estoppel* in science. Continuing scrutiny is always available and the jury can be brought back in at any time when new data becomes available.

The major distinction between legal determinations and scientific assertions lies in the concept of certainty. The legal concept of causation is deterministic: it is an expression of the fiction of certainty, an absolute concept. The scientific concept of causation is probabilistic: it is an expression of the uncertainty of truth, an asymptotic concept.

References

[1] *Sindell*, at 594-95
[2] *Sindell*, at 596
[3] *Sindell*, at 611-12
[4] *Chester* [5]
[5] *Chester* [7]

External links

- Causation in the Law (http://plato.stanford.edu/entries/causation-law) entry by Antony Honoré in the *Stanford Encyclopedia of Philosophy*

Article Sources and Contributors

Roe v Minister of Health *Source*: http://en.wikipedia.org/w/index.php?title=Roe_v_Minister_of_Health *Contributors*: Avalon, David91, Mais oui!, Matilda, Mira, Pearle, PullUpYourSocks, Sirlanz, Tevildo, Tim!, Wikidea, 7 anonymous edits

Court of Appeal of England and Wales *Source*: http://en.wikipedia.org/w/index.php?title=Court_of_Appeal_of_England_and_Wales *Contributors*: Aesopos, Alesueur, Andrew Yong, Angela, BD2412, Camhusmj38, Colenso, Cutler, Cyclopaedic, Davidkinnen, Ddye, Devatipan, Douglas the Comeback Kid, FedLawyer, Francis Davey, Gabbe, Galaxiaad, ISTB351, Icairns, Ironholds, Ironman1104, It Is Me Here, Jezzabr, Jpbowen, KimiSan, Listmeister, Lockesdonkey, Lord Emsworth, Magioladitis, Malcolma, Man vyi, Mathew5000, Mintguy, Mullet, Necrothesp, Ohconfucius, Oleg Alexandrov, Paulmallon, PierreAbbat, Piotrnikitin, Proteus, PullUpYourSocks, Rodhullandemu, Rrius, StAnselm, TaerkastUA, The Super Bean, TheAMmollusc, Tim!, Tom Yates, X76trombones, Жељко Тодоровић, 51 anonymous edits

English tort law *Source*: http://en.wikipedia.org/w/index.php?title=English_tort_law *Contributors*: Anticipation of a New Lover's Arrival, The, Bamkin, Chase me ladies, I'm the Cavalry, CommonsDelinker, D-Rock, David91, Douglas the Comeback Kid, DrFrench, Eastlaw, Edward, Fitzwilliam, Francium12, GeeJo, Ground Zero, HJ Mitchell, IanOfNorwich, Ironholds, JHunterJ, Justjennifer, Kappa, Lambiam, Lame Name, LilHelpa, Mais oui!, Martinp23, Michael Hardy, Mild Bill Hiccup, Myfavoritetort, Nave.notnilc, Neelix, ONEder Boy, Peter Chastain, Piotrnikitin, Puffin, PullUpYourSocks, Rachel2462, RichsLaw, Rjwilmsi, Steamroller Assault, Subzerosmokerain, Tabletop, Toussaint, UHT, Whoop whoop pull up, Wikibofh, Wikidea, Xmts, 34 anonymous edits

Common law *Source*: http://en.wikipedia.org/w/index.php?title=Common_law *Contributors*: "Country" Bushrod Washington, 203.109.250.xxx, 28421u2232nfenfcenc, 66.41.125.xxx, 7, 8charlie0, A Train, A.R., ABCD, AaronSw, Abductive, Acsenray, Acwilson9, Adamjackson77, Adjusting, Aeromix, Agnosticaphid, Agradman, Ahoerstemeier, Akjar13, Aksis, Alaniaris, Alex756, AlexaxelA, Amaher, Andonic, Andre Engels, Andres, Andrew Gwilliam, Andy4226uk, Andy85719, AndyJones, Andycjp, Angrynative, Aniloadam, AnnaFrance, Antandrus, Anthonzi, Antigravityece, Anton Diaz, Anythingyouwant, Arch dude, Arch8887, Arthur Rubin, Ascrivens, Aude, AxSkov, Axlrosen, BD2412, BMF81, Barneyg, Basalisk, BaseTurnComplete, Basejumper9, BasilSorbie, Bblurkin, Bcappella, Bcorr, Bender235, Benwing, Bkonrad, Black85ball, Blaxthos, Blaylockjam10, Bless sins, Bletch, Blue-Haired Lawyer, Boldymumbles, Boleyn, Bongwarrior, Bookish.blogger, Bornintheguz, Bostonian Mike, BrayanGeovanny, Brian Crawford, Brighterorange, BritishWatcher, Brock, Bruce Hall, Bryan Derksen, Brycen, Bryonmorrigan, Btwied, Bwmcmaste, Calanen, Calvin 1998, Can't sleep, clown will eat me, Canjth, CanonLawJunkie, CapitalR, Capricorn42, CaribDigita, Catgut, Ceranthor, Cethegus, Charles8854, Charlesbstewart, Chart123, Chaser, ChicSpandex, Chie one, Chirag, Cholling, Chris the speller, Chris97531, Chrism, Christian118218, Cjmnyc, Closedmouth, Confession0791, Conversion script, Cookiehead, Coolcaesar, Count Truthstein, Cpl Syx, Cquan, Credema, Creidieki, Crust, Cutler, Cvaneg, Cyan, Cyclopaedic, Cynicism addict, DLH, DO'Neil, DaeX, Dale Arnett, Damph, Dan100, Dan6hell66, Dantadd, Darthgriz98, Dave souza, Davewho2, David.Monniaux, David3156, Davidiad, Dbl418, Dchoffman, Dcs.nsw, Delldot, Denisarona, Deplano, DerHexer, Derek Ross, Dereye, Deseavers, DesertFly3, Djk3, Dolovis, Dominic.sedghi, Donarreiskoffer, Doomaangry, Doric Loon, Doug, Douglas the Comeback Kid, Dpr, Dwp2000, Dycedarg, Dylan, Dzsi, ENeville, Eastlaw, Ebehn, Ed g2s, Edward, El C, Elchupalla, Elostirion, Enrico Dirac, Epbr123, Equilibrial, Erianna, Ericamick, Ernstk, Espoo, Esuhl, Evercat, Faigl.ladislav, Falcon Kirtaran, Famspear, Fantilein, Fart in your face!, FasterPussycatWooHoo, Finavon, Flewis, Flex, Flibjib8, Flockmeal, Forever Dusk, Francs2000, Fredrik, Fsol, Funnyhat, GCarty, Garrison Roo, Garrisonroo, George Burgess, GeorgeLouis, GideonF, Gilderien, GinaDana, Gkearns2010, GoShow, Gobbleswoggler, Gojomo, Golgi, Grafen, Graham87, Grametes, Ground Zero, Guanaco, Guppy313, Gzuckier, HDrake, HJ Mitchell, Haham hanuka, Hairy Dude, Harjk, Harthacanute, Headbomb, Hegh, Hemmer, Heron, HighKing, Hiitsme2, Hmains, Hunnjazal, Hydrargyrum, Hydriotaphia, I1abnrk, Iamoldgregg, IanOfNorwich, Igiffin, Ihcoyc, ImhotepBallZ, Imjustmatthew, Incidious, IncognitoErgoSum, Inglorious Busters, Insanity Incarnate, Int21h, Intchanter, Inter, Isaaccp, IsambardBrunel, Ishikawa Minoru, Isis, J.delanoy, J36miles, J8079s, JASpencer, JBC3, JW1805, Jacius, Jackfork, JacobTrue, Jagged 85, JakartaDean, Jalwikip, Jan1nad, JayJasper, Jayzames, JeremyR, Jersyko, Jerzy, Jimmy0103, Jlittlet, Jobbus McKnockey, JohnLai, Johnleemk, Johnuniq, Jon Roland, JonathanFreed, Josephlaumei, Josh3580, Jprg1966, Jrkarp, Jrt989, Jthill, Justflmng, Kahn, Kaihsu, Kaldari, Karenjc, Karl Dickman, Kay Sieverding, Kbh3rd, Kdau, Kelisi, Kenyon, Kgaughan, Khazar2, King of Hearts, Kingnicholas, Kithira, Kizor, Knowledge Seeker, Knuckles, Koavf, Kubanczyk, Kurando, Kwdavids, L33tminion, La Pianista, La goutte de pluie, Lacrimosus, Lambiam, Lawpro, Lemming, Lemonade100, Lenin and McCarthy, Leoshadow2, Leridan, Leszek Jańczuk, Lightmouse, Lizby, Lockesdonkey, Lord Pistachio, Lordmetroid, Lottamiata, Lugnad, Luk, Luna Santin, MBRZ48, MER-C, MJLRGS, Magioladitis, Mais oui!, Malleus Fatuorum, Mandarax, MarcoAurelio, Mark Arsten, MarkGallagher, Markdask, MarnetteD, Martynas Patasius, Masonic, Masterrows, Mathonius, Mathwhiz4444, Matthewi, Maurice Carbonaro, Mcarling, Mdebets, Mediran, Meyer, Mgmillward, Mholland, Michael Hardy, Minimiscience, Minnesotarepublic, Mkcimini, Mm40, Mo0, Modulatum, Mogism, Monkygo, Mootros, Mr Serjeant Buzfuz, Mr. XYZ, MrChandmari, Mslana, Murry1975, N6n, NAHID, NCurse, Nabla, Naelphin, Nat Krause, Nate1481, Naudefj, NawlinWiki, Ncmvocalist, Neorock, Netesq, Neutrality, Neverquick, NewEnglandYankee, Niceguyedc, Nichalp, Noah.eliyasi, Nolelover, Not the quiet type, Notuncurious, Nravi00, Nsaa, Oatmealo, Ohconfucius, Ohnoitsjamie, Okj579, Olegwiki, Oliverkroll, Olly150, One Salient Oversight, OrangeDog, Oscar Coen, Otterpops, Outriggr, Oxymoron83, PJM, PTiger1985, Paddles, PaulGS, Petr Matas, Pgk, Philip Trueman, Pietrow, Pinkadelica, Polluxian, Poorsod, Postdlf, ProhibitOnions, R'n'B, RBBrittain, RL0919, RP459, Raf45Martinez, Ray Van De Walker, Red Bowen, Red Victory, ReluctantPhilosopher, Ret.Prof, Retired username, RexNL, Rich Farmbrough, RjCan, Rjwilmsi, Roadrunner, Robert K S, Rocket000, Roke, Rotbloodi, Rsutphin, RussBlau, RyHarris, S.Örvarr.S, SDC, SWAdair, Samyam, San de Berg, SasiSasi, Saturn star, Scientus, Sciurinæ, Sderose, Seeve, Seudo, Sextus, Sg2002, Shadowjams, Shino Baku, Simeon H, SimonArlott, SimonP, Siroxo, Sixty Hurtz, Skarebo, SkyWalker, Sm351, SmallRepair, Snezzy, Sole Soul, Sourside21, Spb01, SpikeToronto, Splash, Srobak, Starcaster, Starwalk3r, Steven J. Anderson, Stevertigo, Stickee, Storkk, StradivariusTV, SusanLai, Svick, Swampyank, Taejo, Tasc, Tcncv, Teemu Leisti, Texasnole, The Rationalist, The Thing That Should Not Be, TheMidnighters, ThePlaidRanger, Thedoc44, Thingg, Thirty-seven, Thomas Blomberg, Tide rolls, Tim1357, Tim1965, Timesequel, Timofthenorth, Tmh, Tobby72, Tobiasaf, Tomchiukc, TonyBallioni, Tpbradbury, Trabisrox, Tsunaminoai, Tuleytula, Tweek0706, Ty683g542, Ukexpat, Unitedmortgagefunding, Unschool, Uusitunnus, Valkyryn, VampWillow, Vanis314, Vanished User 1004, Vanished user fwefklkaskwi4r592uofmoaihr, Vaquero100, Velho, Veluet, Venu62, Veritastruthemet, Vero.Verite, Vgranucci, Waerloeg, Wal mart store, Walshga, Wavelength, Wayne Slam, Wbray123, Who, Widr, Wik, WikiDao, WikiPedant, Wikid77, Wikidea, Wikiliki, Wikipelli, Will Beback, Woohookitty, WurzelT, Xlation, Yaf, Yakoo, Yamamoto Ichiro, Yendor1958, Yllosubmarine, Zadcat, Zocky, Zoe, Zoroastro, Zpb52, Zro, Zymurgy, Zzuuzz, Île flottante, سادینوئل, 1033 anonymous edits

Cinchocaine *Source*: http://en.wikipedia.org/w/index.php?title=Cinchocaine *Contributors*: 777sms, Andersonblog, Anypodetos, Arcadian, Beetstra, Biscuittin, Casforty, ChemNerd, DavidP73, DiverDave, Dlh-stablelights, Fvasconcellos, Hydro, Louisajb, Pashihiko, Stone, Tevildo, Toyokuni3, حسن علي البط, 5 anonymous edits

Lumbar puncture *Source*: http://en.wikipedia.org/w/index.php?title=Lumbar_puncture *Contributors*: Adavidw, Alex.tan, AllenZh, Almazi, Alro, Alvis, Anthonyhcole, Arcadian, Axl, Azaeov, Babelfish007, Bender235, Bird, Bobblewik, Bobjgalindo, Brainhell, Brandon, CarolGray, Celique, Christian75, Colonies Chris, Crazy Young Spciurkling, Cyclonenim, Darrien, Decoratrix, EamonnPKeane, EhJJ, Eras-mus, Facts707, Faigl.ladislav, Furrykef, Gagandeepjadhav26, Gaius Cornelius, Gchandy, GeeJo, Gidip, Gilberthorpe, Haeinous, Hooperbloob, Hoverflysmiles, Hu12, Hyacinth, Iain southern, Ianmaitland, Ikkyu2, Ilai, Immunize, Iridescent, J04n, Jbmemarbles, Jdchamp31, Jfdwolff, Jmh649, Jsmaye, Karada, Kenneth.jh.han, Kharateez, KingCuongL, Kkailas, Kosebamse, Kwiki, LeaveSleaves, Lipothymia, Lucien504, Lynntyler, MER-C, Maximus Rex, McGeddon, Melah Hashamaim, Mikael Häggström, Mike2vil, MoraSique, Myscrnnm, Nicolas Perrault III, Nikai, Nunh-huh, Nuno Tavares, Oz1sej, Pgrote, Ph.eyes, PierreAbbat, Pkoetters, Polarlys, Preacherdoc, QASIMARA, RaseaC, Ratznium, Reginmund, Remedios44, RexNL, Rickterp, Rob.weitemeyer, Rror, Rubik-wuerfel, SCEhardt, Sam Hocevar, Samuel Siu, SaskatchewanSenator, Seanwmoore, Sep102, Sladen, Smalljim, SteinbDJ, TaintedMustard, TheLou75, Thedreamdied, Theprowier, Timaster735, TotoBaggins, Triesault, Tumadoireacht, Turian, Una Smith, Ursa Gamma, Wolfgang Kufner, Wouterstomp, Xenon chile, Þjóðólfr, 136 anonymous edits

Paraplegia *Source*: http://en.wikipedia.org/w/index.php?title=Paraplegia *Contributors*: A E Francis, Abdull, Acroterion, Adavishambleton, Alan Liefting, Anetode, Arcadian, Arkiedragon, Bentfroggy, Beta m, BiT, Billymac00, Biosthmors, Birczanin, Blanchardb, Blue520, Bobo192, Bongwarrior, Btl, CPTHAWK, CameoAppearance, Cgingold, Ched, Chinju, Cwmhiraeth, CyLMH, DRosenbach, Damian Yerrick, Dannycas, Delldot, Delldot on a public computer, DiverDave, DivineAlpha, Dogah, Drphilharmonic, Dycedarg, Eleassar, Emperorbma, EronMain, EvelinaB, EyeMD, Fabiform, Fminow, Foxj, Fæ, Geraldshields11, Gilliam, Glen, Gordonjcp, Graham87, Gtstricky, Hananekosan, HisSpaceResearch, Horkana, Hydro, Ian Pitchford, Ihasashuvel, J.delanoy, Japanese Searobin, Jfdwolff, Jmarchn, Jmh649, Juhan RSA, Kamicase, Kasten89, Kaykohlman, KieranKiwiNinja, Kikodawgzzz, Kitch, KlappCK, Kwyjibear, Lankiveil, Lar, Lectonar, Lightmouse, LilHelpa, Lkinkade, Mairi, Marscaro, Mephistophelian, Mepolypse, Mishahu, Molerat, Movielover1112, MrFish, MrOllie, Mseliw, MuZemike, Multixfer, Mwanner, NellieBly, NorwegianBlue, Nukervald, Off2riorob, Ohnoitsjamie, Omnipaedista, Paul A, Peaceoutside, Peripitus, Phantomsteve, PrincessofLlyr, RDBrown, RainbowOfLight, Raven4x4x, Ronz, Root4(one), Ruakh, Sammyd41, SapphireSkies, Sarilox, SchfiftyThree, Scohoust, SimonP, Skarebo, Slgordon3, Sole Soul, Steven Zhang, TenPoundHammer, Tesi1700, The Timid Crusader, Theaflaum, Thebeachcowboy, Thmacmill, Tooga, Travelbird, Vary, WBardwin, WLU, Wavelength, Wikieditor1988, Woohookitty, Worky worky, Zigger, דוד55, 276 anonymous edits

Standard of care *Source*: http://en.wikipedia.org/w/index.php?title=Standard_of_care *Contributors*: Andeggs, AvicAWB, BD2412, Cascam1, Chris the speller, Dreftymac, Emeraude, Foofighter20x, JPG-GR, Jeffgolin, Jmunroo, Jokestress, Jsfouche, Kgaughan, LilHelpa, Lkinkade, Misterx2000, Muhandes, Neutrality, Non Curat Lex, PullUpYourSocks, R'n'B, Rfc1394, Robofish, Sardanaphalus, Seidenstud, Splendid1, Thiseye, Txwikinger, Túrelio, Una Smith, Utcursch, WhatamIdoing, Wtshymanski, 23 anonymous edits

Duty of care in English law *Source*: http://en.wikipedia.org/w/index.php?title=Duty_of_care_in_English_law *Contributors*: Allens, AnkhMorpork, AnnaFrance, BD2412, Dancter, Danward, David91, Eastlaw, Epbr123, Francium12, Immunize, JHunterJ, Janus Shadowsong, John of Reading, Mauls, Ninetyone, Nuge, Ospalh, Quiddity, RichsLaw, Ryulong, SCB '92, Selket, SteinbDJ, TheAMmollusc, Twp, Welsh, Wikidea, 40 anonymous edits

Breach of duty in English law *Source*: http://en.wikipedia.org/w/index.php?title=Breach_of_duty_in_English_law *Contributors*: Auric, BD2412, Betacommand, Cutler, David91, Eastlaw, Funkstar86, Iridescent, Jeepday, Khazar2, Leszek Jańczuk, Piotrnikitin, RichsLaw, Shirt58, Stewartdunn, Txwikinger, Wikidea, 11 anonymous edits

Reasonable person *Source*: http://en.wikipedia.org/w/index.php?title=Reasonable_person *Contributors*: AThing, Alex756, Amita999, Andrew Gray, Arctic.gnome, Ardric47, Avb, Barticus88, Bbankos, Benjaminchiang, Bobblewik, Bongwarrior, Brodsky2809, CarolGray, Chaser, Cognita, Cutler, Cyan, Darklilac, Darkwind, Darryle17, Davecrosby uk, Dcoetzee, Dekimasu, Deknowles,

Disambigutron, Douglas the Comeback Kid, Dpr, Dreftymac, Dying, Eastlaw, Egg Centric, ElectricRay, Eyal0, Famspear, Fintor, Foofighter20x, Frecklefoot, Gregbard, Guy Montag, Hakluyt bean, Haukurth, Iridescent, Itschris, JPG-GR, James500, Jeff3000, JonathanSG, Keitei, Kosebamse, Leszek Jańczuk, Mattisse, Maximus Rex, Mdmalon, Michael Hardy, Microfrost, Mkmcconn, Movieshowstopper, Muhandes, NERIC-Security, Neutrality, Non Curat Lex, NuclearWarfare, PBS, PRL42, Pbmaise, Phil Sandifer, Piotrnikitin, Quest for Truth, Ratherthanlater, Robomanx, Sarterus, Sergen McGroth, Shawn D., SimonTrew, Stocksy, Timc, Tobacman, Tregoweth, VampWillow, Vancouverguy, Vapier, Velho, Voidxor, Vzbs34, Wermsker, Wikieditor1988, Woohookitty, Yachtsman1, ישׁ דוד, , 68 anonymous edits

Causation (law) *Source*: http://en.wikipedia.org/w/index.php?title=Causation_%28law%29 *Contributors*: Agradman, Aldux, Amcfreely, Andy85719, Blue-Haired Lawyer, Cantaloupe2, Cjthellama, DVD R W, David.Mestel, David91, Drae, Dying, Flurrysome, Foofighter20x, Funandtrvl, Graeme Bartlett, Grayshi, Grebenkov, Greenlakes, Gregbard, Hmrox, Ironholds, Jeffgolin, Jeremybrennan, Joehubris, LarryBH, Mais oui!, Mandarax, Manicsleeper, Materialscientist, Mattisse, McSly, Miyokan, MrKIA11, Neo-Jay, Omnipaedista, PhilKnight, Philosopher, Pinar, Pjb56, Plutonium27, Quanticle, Reedy, Rich257, Rjwilmsi, Robert Neale, Sardanaphalus, Savant13, Shamesspwns, Sir Nicholas de Mimsy-Porpington, Sir Paul, Skier Dude, Ugur Basak, Very trivial, Wikidea, Wikieditor1988, Yotwen, Yworo, 71 anonymous edits

Image Sources, Licenses and Contributors

File:Royal courts of justice.jpg *Source*: http://en.wikipedia.org/w/index.php?title=File:Royal_courts_of_justice.jpg *License*: unknown *Contributors*: Billinghurst, FlickrLickr, FlickreviewR, Madmedea, Man vyi, Palosirkka, Para

File:Grapevinesnail 01.jpg *Source*: http://en.wikipedia.org/w/index.php?title=File:Grapevinesnail_01.jpg *License*: unknown *Contributors*: Jürgen Schoner

File:Tyldesley miners outside the Miners Hall during the 1926 General Strike.jpg *Source*: http://en.wikipedia.org/w/index.php?title=File:Tyldesley_miners_outside_the_Miners_Hall_during_the_1926_General_Strike.jpg *License*: unknown *Contributors*: Edward, JackyR, Jza84, Man vyi

Image:LegalSystemsOfTheWorldMap.png *Source*: http://en.wikipedia.org/w/index.php?title=File:LegalSystemsOfTheWorldMap.png *License*: unknown *Contributors*: Aldaron, C.Löser, CRGreathouse, Cassowary, Conscious, David Kernow, Dsmurat, Eugrus, Herbythyme, Htonl, J intela, Javitomad, Jayvan, Littledogboy, Maphobbyist, MendozaMX, Munci, Nobelium, Pseudomoi, Ran, RedCoat, SPQRobin, Saguamundi, Santosga, Satesclop, WhisperToMe, Wikiliki, 7 anonymous edits

Image:Constitution of India.jpg *Source*: http://en.wikipedia.org/w/index.php?title=File:Constitution_of_India.jpg *License*: unknown *Contributors*: Calligraphy by Prem Behari Narain Raizda, illuminated by Nand Lal Bose.

File:WilliamBlackstone.jpg *Source*: http://en.wikipedia.org/w/index.php?title=File:WilliamBlackstone.jpg *License*: unknown *Contributors*: User:Felagund

File:Yes check.svg *Source*: http://en.wikipedia.org/w/index.php?title=File:Yes_check.svg *License*: unknown *Contributors*: Anomie

File:Spinal needles.jpg *Source*: http://en.wikipedia.org/w/index.php?title=File:Spinal_needles.jpg *License*: unknown *Contributors*: User:Jojo

File:Spinal tap newborn.JPG *Source*: http://en.wikipedia.org/w/index.php?title=File:Spinal_tap_newborn.JPG *License*: unknown *Contributors*: User:Bobjgalindo

File:Meningitis - Lumbar puncture.jpg *Source*: http://en.wikipedia.org/w/index.php?title=File:Meningitis_-_Lumbar_puncture.jpg *License*: unknown *Contributors*: unknown, maybe L.A. Marty, M.D, Kansas City (author of other photographies in this book)

FSC
www.fsc.org
MIX
Papier | Fördert
gute Waldnutzung
FSC® C083411

Kolibri 360 GmbH
Ferdinand-Jühlke-Straße 7
99095 Erfurt, Deutschland
produktsicherheit@kolibri360.de

Druck:
CPI Druckdienstleistungen GmbH
im Auftrag der
Kolibri 360 GmbH
Ferdinand-Jühlke-Str. 7
99095 Erfurt